Authentic
Living

Blessings!

Herb

LUMINAIRE STUDIES

Authentic Living

BRINGING BELIEF AND LIFESTYLE TOGETHER

Studies in James

HERB KOPP

WINNIPEG, MB CANADA

HILLSBORO, KS USA

KINDRED
PRODUCTIONS

AUTHENTIC LIVING: BRINGING BELIEF AND LIFESTYLE TOGETHER
Copyright 1996 by Kindred Productions, Winnipeg, MB Canada

Published simultaneously by Kindred Productions, Winnipeg, Manitoba R2L 3E5 and
Kindred Productions, Hillsboro, Kansas 67063

Cover design by TS Design Associates, Winnipeg
Book design by Fred Koop, Winnipeg
Printed in Canada by The Christian Press, Winnipeg

Canadian Cataloguing in Publication Data
Kopp, Herbert, 1941 -

Authentic living

(Luminaire studies)
Includes bibliographical references.
ISBN 0-921788-33-9

1. Bible. N.T. James - Commentaries. I. Title.
II. Series.

BS2785.3.K67 1996   227 ' .91077   C96-920085-4

International Standard Book Number: 0-921788-33-9

TABLE OF CONTENTS

INTRODUCTION

Beginning Matters

James, a servant of God and of the Lord Jesus Christ, To the twelve tribes scattered among the nations: Greetings (James 1:1).

The small Epistle of James, only 108 verses in total, has had a long, difficult history finding acceptance as a legitimate part of the biblical canon. In its early life it was either relatively unknown or simply ignored by the early church fathers. Tertullian, one of the third century church fathers whose writings are full of biblical references, 7,258 in all, does not quote from James at all. When it was finally included in the biblical canon, it was accepted either grudgingly or with considerable hostility. Clearly this epistle has not been accorded a central place in the life of the church.

The church is poorer for its neglect of this book. Although it does not articulate the primary foundational premises of a Christologically centered faith as Paul's letters do, it still has a powerful message for the church. It argues strongly for an authentic Christian lifestyle and witness.

The church is always in danger of emphasizing one facet of the faith over another. The 20th century evangelical church has frequently been more concerned about maintaining kerygmatic confessional faithfulness than ethical faithfulness. It has not intentionally chosen belief over lifestyle; rather it has rightly been concerned with discovering and maintaining the belief system, arguing that if belief is compromised then all is lost. But the heat of the conflict for confessional integrity and faithfulness, it has tended to neglect the ethical side of faith. So it should not surprise us that James has been relegated to the lesser position in the New Testament with the primary focus being on Jesus and Paul.

The perceived weakness of this little book is its apparent softness on the kerygma, the fact that it is not structured like Paul's letters and its underemphasis of the confessional aspect of the Gospel. Many readers of James would be more comfortable if the ethical exhortations would flow from a strong Christological premise as it does in Romans, Galatians and Ephesians. James' style, however, should not detract from what the Holy Spirit is saying to the church. This epistle's strength is that it calls the people of God in a direct straightforward manner to bring belief and lifestyle together. It does this forcefully and uncompromisingly, almost shouting at the reader through the use of the imperative mood which is used more than 60 times in this brief writing. It is concerned almost entirely with how the church is to live within the community of believers and within the world.

By relegating this epistle to a lesser position in the canon and within the life of the church, Christians have become impoverished. The church desperately needs the words and wisdom of this missive to create a faithful people of God who not only believe the correct way but also live the right way.

The Epistle of James is particularly important for the Anabaptist tradition of the church which has kept alive the dream of the radical reformers who understood discipleship to be the integration of belief with life. When Menno Simons wrote:

> A true evangelical faith cannot lie sleeping for it clothes the naked, it comforts the sorrowful, it gives the hungry food and it shelters the destitute (*Sing Alleluia*, Kindred Press, p. 111).

he was setting out his understanding of "the way of Jesus" who calls all followers to embrace a belief which issues in a life of bold Christian action. A church that does not call itself to ethical faithfulness is not a faithful church. A church that prides itself in holding to the correct belief system but does not integrate this into good works as the normative outworking of its faith is a wayward and weak church.

In a day when it is fashionable to see things in terms of priorities rather than wholeness, it is easy to fall into the trap of overemphasizing one truth at the expense of another; for example, worship, social action, evangelism, the Holy Spirit or end-time eschatology. Rather than holding two or more important truths in tension, the church has frequently become mesmerized by current popular trends. The church needs to be reminded it is not more of one and less of the other; rather it needs balance so all facets of the Christian experience are understood and practiced. The Epistle of James ought not to be ignored. It is an important part of the canonical puzzle as it helps to set a direction for the church, a direction which calls the church to consistent Christian living lest it speak in one way but live another way.

AUTHORSHIP: WHICH JAMES?

The epistle begins with the simple introductory sentence: "James, a servant of God and of the Lord Jesus Christ." This suggests that "James" was well enough known to his readers that no additional biographical material was necessary to identify him.

The name James was a very common Hebrew nomenclature. The name which we have translated as James (Iakobus) in our text can also be translated Jacob. There are five persons by this name in the Scriptures (and a sixth person is added simply to show how far some commentators go in trying to find the author of this letter) who become candidates for writing this epistle.

Jacob the Patriarch. Several scholars have argued this is the work of Jacob, the Old Testament patriarch. It is suggested this letter is to be seen as an allegorical writing concerning his 12 sons and their relationships toward one another and those of the surrounding culture. This can be readily dismissed and is mentioned only to show how far some scholars go to determine the authorship of this writing.

An unknown James. Martin Luther, among others, has suggested this letter to be the work of an unknown author. The strength of this view, as well as its weakness, is that it might be any of the many persons named James. For those who do not think this epistle worthy of apostolic authority given its content and style, this view allows for an easy explanation of its curious content and manner of writing. For example, Martin Luther did not think too highly of this epistle and therefore might have not wanted it in the biblical canon. Such a view would also safeguard the reputation of James the Just, the noteworthy Jerusalem church leader, to whom the authorship is usually attributed.

However, for those who argue that the introductory statement reflects a churchman so well-known that no other introductory material was necessary, the idea of an unknown James as author is problematic and unacceptable.

James, the son of Zebedee, the brother of John. We meet this James again and again in the Scriptures. He was called by Jesus to be a disciple (Matt. 4:21-22); he is named in the list of disciples (Matt. 10:2); he was present with John and Peter on the Mount of Transfiguration (Matt. 17:1); and he was present with the Lord in his hour of passion in Gethsemane just moments before his arrest (Matt. 26:37).

James, the son of Zebedee, the brother to John, was executed by King Herod Agrippa (Acts 12:1-2) likely between A.D. 41-43. This early death seems to rule out this James as the author of this epistle.

James, the son of Alphaeus. Very little is known concerning this James except that he was one of the chosen disciples of Jesus (Matt. 10:3). Although this does not necessarily rule out his authorship of the epistle, since nothing is also known about Jude who authored the letter which bears his name, it does make it highly improbable that he is the author.

James the Little (or the Lesser), or the Younger. Of this James we know very little except that his parentage and family members are named in the New Testament. His mother was Mary, the wife of Clopas, and he had a brother named Joses (Mark 15:40). Many commentators think this James and the previously discussed James, the son of Alphaeus to be the same person. If this is the case, and there appears to be some evidence for it, his authorship must be dismissed for the same reasons.

James, the brother of our Lord. This James was a very well-known person. Although he has come to be known as James the Just in scholarly writings, in the biblical narrative he is simply known as James. Paul identifies him as "James, the Lord's brother" (Gal. 1:19) whom he visited in Jerusalem after his three-year hiatus in Arabia.

As a younger person James did not believe in Jesus (John 7:3-5) and he is known to have had at least three brothers and some sisters (Mark 6:3). Nothing is known about his conversion but he quickly rose to prominence in the Jerusalem church. When Peter was miraculously released from prison (Acts 12:1ff) and appeared at Mary's front door, he told the praying house-church to go "tell James and the brothers" about this (Acts 12:17), indicating the prominence to which James had already risen in the Jerusalem church community.

By the time the Council in Jerusalem had been convened, James had developed sufficient stature and theological acumen to listen carefully to the arguments presented by Peter, Paul and Barnabas (Acts 15:1ff) and to propose a summation that was to become the basis for unified Christian action.

After returning to Jerusalem from his third extensive trip to the west, Paul was joyfully received by the church. On the next day, Paul went to meet James and the elders and reported to them "what the Lord had done among the Gentiles" (Acts 21:17ff). Paul acknowledges James, together with Peter and John, to be the pillars who extended to him and Barnabas " the right hand of fellowship" (Gal. 2:9).

Obviously this James, also called James the Just, was well enough known to open this writing with the simple words "James, a servant of God", and be immediately recognized and identified. Some scholars have suggested that an anonymous person may have borrowed the name James to give credence to this writing and then passed it off as coming from James the Just. However, if this were the case, the fraudulent writer would have likely been careful to enhance the biographical data to give it the appearance of authenticity. After all, this epistle is one of the very few which opens with such a short identifying statement. The Letter of Jude and the Epistle to the Hebrews are the other exceptions, with Hebrews having no introduction.

Other objections to James the Just as author are more serious. First, some argue the Greek is too good for a Jewish person who had grown up in Nazareth of Galilee. The writing also reflects an idiomatic Greek, suggesting the author was steeped in the cultural and linguistic nuances of the Greek world. Where did James, who spent most of his life, if not all of it, in Palestine learn not only fluent Greek but good idiomatic Greek?

Second, the scant Christological content of the letter is strange. Only twice (1:1; 2:1) is Christ named. While a Christological understanding pervades the underlying assumptions of the author, the absence of reference to Christ seems curiously strange. This strangeness is further emphasized in that James is "the Lord's brother", and although not necessarily an eyewitness to most of the events of Jesus' life, he most certainly would have known of them.

Not only is there an absence in naming Christ, there is also a well-noted absence of the kerygma of the early church - the life, death, resurrection and imminent return of the Lord. James is a very God-centred book. God is named more than 20 times. The frequent use of "the Lord", following the Hebrew custom of not naming God, usually refers to God rather than Christ. Also, "the Lord of Sabaoth," a favorite designation of Old Testament writers, is introduced to the New Testament in this epistle. The only other New Testament occurrence of this title is when Paul quotes Isaiah 1:9 in Romans 9:29.

Third, the law is treated in a Jewish way in this writing. It is celebrated as "the law of liberty" and "the royal law". This is clearly in tension with the rest of the New Testament writing which sees law in terms of bondage. All of the illustrations are from the lives of Old Testament persons (Abraham, Rahab, Job, Elijah), while the life and actions of Jesus Christ are never used for role-model purposes.

Fourth, the most seriously noted difference which questions the authorship of James the Just is the perceived conflict between James and Paul on the subject of faith and works. The Acts narrative leaves no doubt that Paul and James knew each other well. They were agreed on the meaning of the newness which the Christ-event had inaugurated. They had a common understanding of the Christian kerygma.

Why then do they move in such diverse directions in their writings? Paul's writings are full of Christological statements; James has none. Paul systematically outlines the tension between grace and law, and centers the Christian faith squarely in grace as a gift; James hardly notes grace but celebrates "the law of liberty".

So who wrote the Epistle of James? Of all the options available, most of the evidence points to James, the Lord's brother, the leader of the Jerusalem church. The obstacles cited above are difficult to answer, but are not overwhelming or impossible to bridge.

Stereotyping the disciples of Jesus as dusty, loudmouthed, uneducated illiterates who were out of touch with the cultural, political and linguistic realities of their day is too simplistic. It makes good copy and it appeals to our senses that the underdog can triumph, but that is not the focus in the New Testament. The Hellenization process, begun in the fourth century B.C. with the invasion of Alexander the Great, had continued unabated for many centuries, interrupted only by the Maccabean era and the Qumran community of Essenes who carried this fight forward into Jesus' day. The overpowering might of the Roman juggernaut and the subtle, seeping influence of the Greek-speaking world had permeated the culture and business milieu of the land. To argue that James, who rose quickly to a place of prominence in the Jerusalem church, was incapable of writing reasonably good Greek places too much emphasis on the origins of his birth and the nature of his upbringing and education.

Regarding the differences between James and Paul, John Calvin, the reformer and contemporary of Martin Luther, brings a more balanced perspective to this epistle which is separate from the rest of the New Testament canon. While acknowledging that it does not answer the question of content nor the Christological versus the Theo-logical center of this writing, it does address the issue with reason. Calvin writes:

> If James seems rather more reluctant to preach the

grace of Christ than an apostle should ..., we must remember not to expect everyone to go over the same
ground. I am fully content to accept this Epistle. It contains nothing unworthy of an apostle (Adamson, p.
164).

A modified view of this position is to interact with the view
proposed by Peter Davids. Davids suggests that all of the material in the epistle is part of the preaching of James; however, an editor at a later date put it into the form it now has. In other words,
this epistle is not fraudulently passed off as the work of James the
Just or an unknown editor; rather it is the preaching of James com-
piled by an editor who was fluent in idiomatic Greek, and then it
was sent in the name of James as a pastoral letter to the church
scattered throughout the Roman Empire.

THE DATE OF THE EPISTLE

Three options are open to us in the dating of this material: an
early date, a late date, and both an early and late date. If James
the Just is the author, we must date it just before A.D. 60, but not
too much after that date. If this is the work of an unknown person named James, the date can be as late as A.D. 130. If we accept
the Peter Davids' idea that the material is the preaching of James
the Just but an editor organized it and sent it to the scattered
church, the range is from A.D. 40 to A.D. 66.

THE FORM OF THE LETTER

Flow-of-consciousness is a 20th century term created to describe a writing style which allows ideas to flow freely from one to
another. Often the only connection between one idea and the following idea is that the first one brought the second to mind. Although this term was not known in the first century, the Epistle of
James seems to be a pristine example of such writing. It has been
suggested by many commentators that the epistle is an example of
Jewish preaching in which the main ideas are noted early in the
homily and then developed by returning to them again and again.

This might explain why James returns to topics such as the need for wisdom, the plight of the disadvantaged, the problem of unruly speech, and the need to bring one's life of good works in line with one's belief.

Often James will open a paragraph with one thought, but instead of pursuing the topic and developing it fully, he jumps to another line of thinking and develops it instead. Sometimes when the reader expects a closing sentence to summarize a reasonably disciplined discourse on a subject, it does not happen; instead, an entirely new idea is advanced.

This epistle is full of surprises, all of them good. It moves at a brisk pace. It has many commands in it and it tends not "to sit on the fence" on any issue. It prods the church and the individual believer to bring belief and lifestyle together. It is truly a word from God for our age, and is well suited to preaching, teaching and personal study because it deals with practical matters and calls for a change in behaviors and lifestyle.

HOW TO USE THIS BOOK

This book is divided into 13 chapters. The first 12 deal specifically with the text; the 13th chapter is a theology of the Epistle of James where all its major teachings are summarized.

Each chapter is divided into five parts. **The Text** is reproduced using the New International Version. This is followed by **The Flow and Form of the Text** which attempts to chart the flow of ideas which comprise the bulk of the text. The unity of the specific text is addressed and where a dramatic shift in the flow-of-consciousness occurs, the reader is alerted to this in advance of determining the meaning of the text. **The Text Explained** addresses the central teaching of the pericope in non-technical language. Greek words are used only when a particularly rich word is used. An attempt is also made to highlight some of the interesting nuances which ooze from the text. The section labeled, **Application, Teaching/Preaching Points** draws practical lessons from each passage of text under scrutiny. Finally, **Personal Response** questions are added to make this book as user-friendly as possible.

CHAPTER ONE

The Opening Salvo: Testing and Trials

Consider it pure joy, my brothers, whenever you face tri-als of many kinds, because you know that the testing of your faith develops perseverance. Perseverance must finish its work so that you may be mature and complete, not lacking anything. If any of you lacks wisdom, he should ask God, who gives generously to all without finding fault, and it will be given to him. But when he asks, he must believe and not doubt, because he who doubts is like a wave of the sea, blown and tossed by the wind. That man should not think he will receive anything from the Lord; he is a double-minded man, unstable in all he does (James 1:2-8).

The Flow And Form of the Text

This paragraph forms the first discreet unit in this epistle. It is introduced by the phrase "My brothers" and concludes with a warning against unbelief. The whole pericope is characterized by a torrent of words which almost overwhelms the reader. In a rapid flow-of-consciousness style of writing, James moves from the central dominant theme of the paragraph to all things that the opening idea brings to mind.

At the heart of this passage is the theme of trials. The blunt opening reinforces the identity of the readers; that is, the community of faith which is in the *diaspora*, which means "scattered" (1:1). Whether these readers are scattered throughout the Roman world by choice or through persecution is hard to determine, but the passage is directed towards a people who are in the midst of trials.

This paragraph revolves around five words: trials, faith, endurance, perfect and wisdom. If we were to summarize this text by constructing a sentence using these five words, it would be as follows: trials require faith, which produces endurance, which makes one perfect, for which we need wisdom.

The Text Explained

There is a very logical progression of thought in this opening paragraph. He begins with immense energy, driven by the pressing urgency to get to the heart of the matter as quickly as possible. With the scantiest of introductions the writer jumps right into the subject matter which is occupying his attention and moves through four phases of thinking.

The problem, the solution and the result (vv.2-4) Phase one highlights three things: the problem is stated; an appropriate attitude toward the problem is counseled; and a positive result may be anticipated if "problem" and "attitude" are brought together.

The problem is the trials, troubles and temptations the scattered people of God are experiencing (1:1). This Greek word *peirasmos* is probably most usefully translated "trials" rather than "temptations", though the idea of temptation is not far removed from it. It is modified by a colorful word which is translated in a variety of ways: multicolored, variegated, various. This word was used to describe the wide-ranging nature of the difficulties and troubles which have befallen the people of God. It can refer to the trials which are simply part of life or to trials and persecutions which come from an outside source. In the case of this epistle, it is probably both. If James is dated later rather than earlier, it can also refer to political oppression from Roman sources.

The attitude the writer encourages in the face of such trials is joy. To catch the significance of what James is saying, many of the newer translations strengthen the more traditional and accurate rendering, "Consider it all joy" (RSV, NASB) with phrases like "Consider it pure joy" (NIV), "count yourselves supremely happy" (REB) or "Consider it a sheer gift" (The Message, 1993). This joyful attitude runs counter to how we expect humanity to behave. Trials and testings are to be resisted, but if they are inevitable and can not be avoided, then at best they are to be tolerated.

The result of bringing a joyful attitude to the problems and trials of life is that steadfastness is produced. Steadfastness, or endurance, is a great New Testament concept. The Greek compound word *hupomone* literally means "to remain under". The word was commonly used to describe a beast of burden, a camel, a donkey or alas a slave who was forced to carry the load to a destination without throwing it off. Just as the beast of burden remains under the load, carrying it fully to its destination, in like manner we are to endure.

Therefore the opening proposition of this paragraph is that trials joyfully borne produce the ability within us to remain under the load and to carry it to our destination without giving up.

The nature of endurance (v. 4) Having given the central theme of this paragraph, James now departs from it by pursuing the nature and character of endurance. He does this by citing the reason why endurance is so important in the Christian life. Endurance is that virtue which allows God to finish and perfect that which must be accomplished within a believer. Endurance is validated by finishing the course, by seeing through to the end that which needs to be brought to completion. In the process of completing the course, James adds, a threefold result will emerge: perfection, completeness and lacking in nothing.

Perfection is often a misunderstood concept. In the English language perfection is the ultimate achievement. It can not be improved upon nor made better. In the Greek culture, perfection *teleios* carries the sense of having achieved what was intended; attaining the end which was planned. In the original writing, "perfect" has a softer meaning. We are perfect when we are mature, when we become that which we are intended to be, when we do what we were created to do. A child is said to be perfect when it has learned to read; runners are perfect when they finish the race; a business person is perfect when the deal is accomplished. There is less emphasis on ultimate achievement than on achieving what was intended and attaining that which was planned. Therefore, in this text having endured to the end or having remained under the load without throwing it off until the destination has been reached is being perfect.

The two complementary words, "complete" and "lacking nothing," simply reinforce the previous idea of having fully achieved that which had been set out at the beginning.

The need for wisdom (v.5) In pursuing the meaning of endurance, a special dilemma has been created for James; perfection, completeness and lacking nothing are qualities which usually lie beyond the reach of humans. Quickly he notes the problem and addresses a solution, found in appealing to God for wisdom.

With the introduction of the idea of wisdom, James puts the reader in touch with the first of many Old Testament concepts. In the Old Testament wisdom has to do with both attitude and action. It is a wide-ranging word with a long, rich history. For example, it can mean the ability to do skillful, artistic work (Ex. 28:3; 31:3); it can mean understanding with insight and prudence (Prov. 3:2; I Chron. 22:12); or it can mean the sagacious behavior which enables a person to master life's complexities (Prov. 8:32-36).

But there is a further meaning which deserves particular attention. The opposite of wisdom in the Old Testament is not so much being unwise or a simpleton as it is being foolish. The essence of foolishness is not having a lack of prudence and understanding; foolishness, in biblical terms is to reject God. Therefore the writers of Old Testament wisdom literature repeatedly make this claim:

> The fear of the Lord is the beginning of knowledge, but
> fools despise wisdom and discipline (Prov. 1:7; 9:10; Job
> 28:28; Ps. 111:10),

and the Psalmist can cry,

> The fool says in his heart, "There is no God"   (14:1;
> 53:1).

To be wise in biblical terms is to keep God in the center of our consciousness and lives. It is both an attitude and an action. So when James frames the problem with the comment, "If any of you lacks wisdom ..." and the self-evident answer comes back immediately, "Of course we do!" he points out that it is very hard to live life well without God being in the center of things. By conceding that all believers need wisdom to live well, James has set the framework for a discussion on how this wisdom will come to the persons requiring it. The reason we need wisdom so badly is because of the complex, multifaceted and multivariegated trials which throw our lives into confusion.

The answer to our need for wisdom is God (vv. 4b-8) The answer to keeping God centered in our lives is quite simple: "Ask God!" The verb *aiteito* which means to ask, is a present continuous tense verb meaning we are always to be asking. The active voice means we ourselves are to do the asking; the imperative mood means we are commanded to do it.

The only condition placed on the person asking is that it is done in faith. Faith in this context is a synonym for believing. The asking must be accompanied by the belief that God will in fact give us this wisdom. The asking, you will notice, is not for the removal of the trial but for endurance to bear it. Such believing touches the heart of a gracious God who will give generously and without begrudging us what we want. On the other hand, to not believe or to not have faith undermines our ability to receive from God the strength to keep God centered in life in the midst of trials. If we refuse to believe that God can give us the strength to endure, we will likely not endure. Therefore it is logical the writer should conclude, "Such a person ought not to think he will receive anything from the Lord" (vs. 7).

Application, Teaching/Preaching Points

This text is rich fare for personal application as well as for teaching and preaching in the church. Five outstanding points can be drawn from this short text.

The inevitability of trials. By using "whenever" rather than "if", the text makes it clear that trials are inevitable. Not all trials have the same face; they are varied, multicolored and variegated. They come in all shapes and sizes; they strike at us in every phase of our life cycle; they come to us with every degree of intensity. Sometimes they are simply part of the trials which come to all of us in the ordinary events of life; other times they come to us from sources outside of our own control because we are part of the scattered people of God.

The gift of endurance. For some the option of how to handle these trials is simply a yes/no matter; for others they are handled on a continuum between the polar opposites of enduring them with joy or fighting them with anger. The attitude we bring to these trials will largely determine our success in handling them. To fight that which is inevitable is folly; however, this text does not encourage an attitude of martyrdom or a negative way of thinking about trials. Believers are not persons who go out of their way to find trials and then rejoice in having found them. Believers are people who, when the trials come, face them squarely and optimistically.

Joy is not to be confused with happiness. Happiness takes its root meaning from the Latin *hap* which means chance, while joy is a fruit of the Spirit (Gal. 5:22). Joy comes to us when we know the presence of God in our lives. It is possible to have a deep abiding joy without necessarily having happiness. Happiness is dependent on circumstances; joy can be present even in the most difficult circumstances of life. Endurance gives joy a chance to flourish and joy gives endurance a chance to grow.

When endurance has done its work through time, it will produce a mature, balanced, complete person. Endurance is the biblical antidote to a culture which wants instant relief from the trauma of life. Endurance tests the quality of our faith-lives and measures whether our belief in God is adequate to accept his sustaining strength which can see us through to the end.

The need for wisdom. All of life is difficult, but it is particularly difficult for those who stubbornly and arrogantly think themselves to be clever enough to live by their own wits. We are blessed and cursed by self-reliance. When the inevitable trials and troubles come, our first impulse usually is towards self-reliance. This makes keeping God in the center of our life difficult. Trials can nudge us toward God when we see him as the sustaining power in the midst of troubles; or trials can drive us away from God when we blame him for that which besets us.

Our need for wisdom is really our need for God. To think of wisdom as simply the ability to work our way through our problems is not enough. To live unwisely is to cut ourselves off from the One who not only gives us wisdom for life, but who is the incarnation of wisdom. To know God is to tap into his wisdom; to reject God is to alienate ourselves from his wisdom.

The necessity of believing prayer. The text is clear and straightforward in its insistence that all one needs to do is "ask God" and he will grant us our petition. At one level this dismantles all mystery from prayer. It is the cry of the heart for courage to endure. In this context asking God is not an appeal to have the burden removed or have us removed from a perplexing situation. In this text there is nothing complicated or hard to understand about prayer. Prayer is asking God for the courage and sustaining strength to endure with joy all those things which have come into our lives. Prayer is asking God to remain in the center of our being through the cycles of good and bad. Prayer is asking God not so much to explain the trials and unfairness of life but to give wisdom to handle the circumstances we can not understand.

The only condition placed on prayer is we must believe. Belief is solely the domain of the believer who trusts God. Believing prayer flows from the believer as naturally as good trees bear good fruit. Believing is not gritting the teeth and forcing oneself to believe that which is impossible to believe. Believing is not only trusting God but placing our unbelief into God's hands (Mark 9:24).

The continuing problems for the double-minded. The text leaves us gasping. This pericope concludes in the strangest way. It warns of the continuing trouble which will beset those who do not keep God centered in all of life. Unbelief creates a self-sustaining cycle of confusion, uncenteredness and double-mindedness. Double-mindedness creates instability which creates more uncenteredness, and God is driven farther from life.

This text teaches there is only one way through the multifaceted trials which are inevitable in life. We must endure our trials with joy asking God for wisdom in living, and believing he will truly come through for us by holding us in his care. Any double-mindedness is incompatible with faith and destroys both endurance and belief.

Personal Response

* The Scriptures are given to lead the individual and church community to God and toward spiritual maturity. The church is present on every continent and in most of the people-groups of the world. DISCUSS: How are the trials which you experience in your lives different from the trials Christians experience in other parts of the world? How does this text relate to your kind of trials and those trials people in other lands experience?

* Prayer is speaking to God about those things which occupy our thinking and our lives. DISCUSS: Is it proper to ask God to take away those things which cause us much alarm and trauma? Is the believer's only option to endure trials with joy? When is it right to ask God to take away a trial?

* Wisdom is a universally sought quality and in our society is understood to be the identifying mark of a decent productive person. No one wants to be unwise. DISCUSS: Is James correct when he insists that wisdom can only come from God? What do you think about all the self-help guides, books and seminars which attempt to lead individuals toward wise, mature living? How is the wisdom which God gives in response to believing prayer different from the wisdom which we can accumulate by other means?

CHAPTER TWO

An Upside-Down Community:
Exaltation and Humiliation

The brother in humble circumstances ought to take pride in his high position. But the one who is rich should take pride in his low position, because he will pass away like a wild flower. For the sun rises with scorching heat and withers the plant; its blossom falls and its beauty is destroyed. In the same way, the rich man will fade away even while he goes about his business (James 1:9-11).

The Flow and Form of the Text

What immediately strikes the reader of this pericope is its strange placement in the overall text. Logically verse 12 and following ought to follow verse 8. If you read 1:2 and then 1:12-18, omitting 1:9-11, the smooth continuation of the line of thought will be noticed. However, this text is inserted right in the middle of a discourse on endurance and trials.

Three questions need to be addressed: how do we explain this strange placement, how is the text constructed and from where do the ideas come?

Here the writing style known as flow-of-consciousness explains the seemingly intrusive paragraph. Flow-of-consciousness in a written document is very much like the conversations in which we engage. We move effortlessly from one subject to the next. While there is some discontinuity in the subject material of the conversation, there is also a remarkable coherence to the whole because one idea gives birth to another idea.

What gives impetus to a change of subject material is a fertile mind which recognizes the implications of what has just been discussed. Here the subject material is the nature of trials and the manner in which the believer ought to navigate through them. The intent of the free flow of ideas is not to create an airtight logical case on a central theme. Rather it shows how unconnected ideas are composed to form a helpful document. Although the ideas are not logically related, they are nonetheless related to each other and thus are fair game for discourse. James seems to engage in such a free flow of ideas. Throughout the epistle, there will frequently be a jolting from one subject to the next with no apparent connection except that one idea has given birth to another idea.

To suggest verses 9-11 are a later addition, mistakenly copied into the text by a scribe and therefore probably not part of the original material of James, is too restrictive in understanding the free flow of ideas.

In 1:2-8 James has already shown a penchant for taking a central idea and allowing his fertile mind to run with it. In the first section, it has taken him from his central argument that trials are inevitable all the way to the problem of being a double-minded person. From there it is a short step to highlighting the dilemma which is created by having wealth and poverty in the church. It might not follow logically but it certainly follows in the free flow of ideas although not so visible in the text itself, there is a coming together around the theme of living wisely. This theme will be pursued later in this chapter.

The text has remarkable internal unity. It begins with contrasting statements: one concerning the rich and the other concerning the poor. Both statements call for a mindset which is exactly the opposite of what is practiced in society where the rich are powerful and strong, while the poor are powerless and downtrodden. What ties these statements together is not only the contrasting of the lowly (*tapeinos*) with the rich (*plousios*), but also the play on the word "lowly" (*tapeinosei*) which is used to describe the intentional posture of humiliation which the rich are to adopt and express.

Next the text draws support from an Old Testament saying from Isaiah 40:7-8 to strengthen the argument for the rich to make adjustments in their lifestyle. In this text the withering plant is contrasted to the word of God which endures forever; in the James text it is used to illustrate the fragility of life and by implication the passing nature of wealth. This same Old Testament text, though not quoted again, will be used later as grounds to argue that life is very fragile (James 4:13-17).

The writer draws on the Old Testament to augment what is clearly the teaching of Jesus, but to whom he does not appeal or quote. Jesus frequently made the point that it is folly to anchor one's life on the fleeting security of wealth (Matt. 6:19-21; Luke 12:13-21; 18:18-27). In his own way James makes the same point and will return to this matter repeatedly with considerable forcefulness (2:1-7; 4:13-5:6).

The Text Explained

This passage opens as suddenly and abruptly as the previous text. Almost without warning the writer moves from double-mindedness to the problems created by having the rich and poor in the same congregation. James turns the conventional thinking concerning wealth and poverty on its head by suggesting a mindset exactly opposite to what exists in society. In parallel statements he puts forward a formula for understanding the nature of true wealth and earthly wealth. They are not the same thing.

The opening statement addresses the *tapeinos* (the poor, the lowly, the humble, the ones without possessions). They are to boast (*kauchastho*). The present tense declares they are to do it continually; the middle voice suggests they are to do it to themselves; and the imperative mood makes it a command. They are to exalt in having been exalted (*huxos*). They have come from nothing into something; what they have come into is from God. The imperative mood of *kauchastho* seems to indicate a reticence by the humble to boast. Poverty is nothing to boast about so these persons have little experience in telling about the good things that are part of their lives.

There is a boasting which is born of arrogance and is always wrong. It flaunts itself shamelessly. It celebrates its own accomplishments, congratulating itself on its own achievements. But there is also a boasting which is honorable. It humbly admits that what it possesses is from God and in boasting raises its voice in praise to God.

The second part of this formula is that the *plousios* (the rich) are to boast (by implication because the word is not repeated) in their *tapeinosei* (humiliation). The intentional use of this word used to describe the poor in verse 9, calls attention to the former state of those who now celebrate their exaltation. In other words, the rich are to become like the poor were, while the poor are to rejoice and exalt in having received status and high position.

Standing in the shadows of this radical proposition is an Old Testament idea which is modified and galvanized in New Testament thinking. YHWH, the God of Israel, has a heart for the poor, the powerless and the disenfranchised. The old covenant, through the institution of the Sabbath year and the Year of Jubilee (Lev. 25:9ff), protected the rights of the poor by not allowing them to be indentured forever to the rich. There were laws about gleaning (Lev. 19:9ff) and about the stranger in their midst (Ex. 22:21). Wealth was not to be centralized into fewer and fewer hands, thereby stripping the poor of the right to a decent life (Amos 4:1ff).

In the New Testament the poor are not only the economically deprived but also the outcasts for whom there is little room in society. Jesus welcomes the poor, the halt, the blind and the lame to his banquet table, giving them status over the rich who have declined his invitation (Mark. 2:18-22). It is poor Lazarus, not Dives, who sits in the bosom of Abraham (Luke 16:19-32). It is the socially unacceptable tax collector who finds forgiveness and entry into God's kingdom (Luke 18:9-14). It is the immoral woman who does the unthinkable by breaking a flask of perfume on Jesus' feet, and finds acceptance and a new life (Luke 7:36-50).

The *plousios* (the rich) are to boast in their *tapeinosei* (humiliation). This is a difficult sentence to interpret. The humiliation which the rich "should take pride in" (NIV) must not be seen as outright condemnation or rejection of riches. Rather, the humiliation comes when the rich admit that the wealth they possess, which gives them power, status and position in society, is powerless in the kingdom of God. The boasting lies in their admission and recognition that God's grace has come to them in spite of their wealth. It transcends their wealth; it places all wealth into perspective.

Wealth has a seductive nature. The concluding sentence of this pericope (1:11b) suggests it can grasp one so powerfully that people become blinded to their own fading (*maranthesetai*) and fail to see it in the midst of their busyness.

Isaiah 40:7-8 is used in an illustrative way. This simile must not be read as a particular judgment on the rich person because all people, regardless of wealth and status, face the ravages of the burning sun. For all of us the "blossom falls and its beauty is destroyed". But for those who recognize their poverty and boast in their newly acquired high position (1:9) or those who have rejected the seductiveness of riches and have come to boast in their humiliation (1:10), the fading of the blossom is not to be feared.

Application, Teaching/Preaching Points

This text has as much relevance for us today as it did for the emerging church in the first century. At the heart of these three verses is the radical nature of the New Testament faith community, the church. The church is quite unlike anything in society. Here all the barriers which divided one human being from another were voided. However, the early church, much like the contemporary church, struggled with the temptation to allow wealth to define a persons' worth and determine their place in the faith community.

Since this is an ongoing problem, we do well to hear the teaching of this text. Three important matters are highlighted for our attention.

The poor and the rich. Attitude plays a significant role in how people view themselves and how they are viewed by others. James addresses this matter forthrightly. The poor and the humble are strongly encouraged to speak about their personal elevation. The rich, who would more naturally be inclined to speak about themselves, their accomplishments and their social standing, are discouraged from flaunting their power and are called to boast in their humiliation - a humiliation that comes from realizing wealth will not give them status with God or a special place within the faith community.

Both the poor and the rich need a change in attitude. If this change does not occur, then the same attitudes which prevail in culture will be mirrored in the church. This radical shift in attitude is to be carried forward equally by both the poor and the rich. If the poor do not have this change burned into their consciousness, they will remain in their lowliness. If the rich do not have this radical change stamped into their lives, they will remain arrogant and aloof from the poor. The loser in both cases will be the faith community.

This attitude change comes only from having been introduced into the faith community that lives by the wisdom which comes from God; that is, having God centered profoundly and deeply in all of life (1:5).

The passing nature of wealth and life. We tend to be a forgetful people and need to be reminded of the important things in life. One area of particular forgetfulness concerns our possessions and mortality. For most of us, acquiring possessions is such an arduous process, we are in danger of staking too much of our lives on its value. The axiom "We don't own our possessions, they own us" is often a self-fulfilling prophesy.

The text loudly and clearly reminds a forgetful people about the fragile, passing nature of life and wealth. Since both are like flowers in a meadow, we ought not to think either has an eternal lifespan. Death comes to both; sometimes suddenly through an early frost, other times simply through the fatigue of autumn. But it does come, and it is inevitable.

The bottom line is we ought not to place ultimate value on that which is, by definition, passing. Wealth passes away; life passes away.

A caution against undiscerning busyness. The text ends with a sad statement. Busyness and the unrestrained pursuit of wealth will blind us to the inevitability of death. The ultimate question in life is not so much what we are willing to die for; rather, what we are willing to live for? This final statement is so all-inclusive it covers more than just the busyness of pursuing wealth, although that is the particular direction the writer takes the argument. It has a much more universal application. It warns that anything which gets in the way of wise living (that is, keeping God centered in life) will mean losing life. And to lose life is to lose all!

Personal Response

   * The rich and the poor have always existed together in society. They are also present in the church. Sometimes there is tension between the opinions the rich offer and the opinions the poor give. DISCUSS: Is the present church guilty of distinguishing between the rich and the poor? Are the wealthy persons in your congregation more influential than the poor persons? What is the answer to equality in this matter?

   * In the Old Testament wealth is a sign of God's favor and blessing; for example, Abraham, Jacob and Job. This Old Testament idea is frequently carried over into our times. DISCUSS: Is wealth still to be seen as a blessing from God? Or is being wealthy a sin? Is it proper for the rich to publicly thank God for their wealth?

   * Our text speaks about the poor exalting in their exalted position and the rich exalting in their humiliation. DISCUSS: How can this be done practically in the church? Does your local congregation have a forum for such activity? If you were to create a public forum for this, how would you shape it?

CHAPTER THREE

Facing Into The Wind: The Bliss Of Endurance

Blessed is the man who perseveres under trial, because when he has stood the test, he will receive the crown of life that God has promised to those who love him (James 1:12).

The Flow and Form of the Text

The third discreet unit of the epistle is a single-sentence summary statement, although it also has the structure and strength to stand alone on its own merit. It is written in a form commonly called a beatitude. Beatitudes are pithy sayings which begin with the word "blessed", then add a virtue which is to be possessed, and conclude with a result that is beneficial to the practitioner. Beatitudes are scattered throughout the Old Testament (Ps. 1:1; 32:1) and New Testament. In the New Testament they sometimes appear as a block of material (Matt. 5:1-12; Luke 6:20-22) or are scattered throughout a book (Rev. 1:3; 14:13; 16:15; 19:9; 20:6; 22:7; 22:14). In the Old Testament the opposite of blessing is "curse". Cursings sometimes appear in lists (Deut. 27:15-26) while blessings usually stand alone. In his treatment of the Sermon on the Plain (Luke 6:20-26) Luke juxtaposes a New Testament pattern of a group of blessings with the Old Testament pattern of a group of curses. In James there is only one beatitude, although the sentiment of 1:12 appears again in 5:11.

Verse 12 is written as a summation, a call to vigilance and a shout of encouragement. This sentence seems to belong more appropriately after 1:8. Take a moment to read 1:2-8 and 1:12, omitting 1:9-11, and you will see how easily it fits into that context but even though it is placed after verse 11, it still acts as a summary statement for what has preceded it.

At the heart of this sentence is the Greek word *hupomone* (per-severance, endurance). This common New Testament word (32 times) appears only three times in this epistle, twice in the open-ing sections and once (5:11) for illustrative purposes. It previous-ly appeared in 1:3 where it is set out as the goal which is achieved through enduring testing with joy. In this second use, the writer takes the virtue of endurance to greater heights than in 1:2-4. James strengthens the virtue of *hupomone* by promising "the crown of life" will be given to its practitioners. With this usage, the writer closes his treatment of the subject except to illustrate Job's enduring patience (5:11).

The Text Explained

The beatitude as it appears in the New Testament has a well-developed form with three distinct parts. The beatitude in our text follows this form. The first is the declaration of blessedness; the second is the virtue to be possessed; and the third is the result.

Blessedness: a bliss beyond happiness. The Greek word *markarios* is usually translated into English as blessed, fortunate and happy. All these words are problematic as none of them fully conveys the meaning of the text. Although *markarios* can rightly be translated "happy" (Jerusalem Bible, Good News Bible) it seems to not have the right nuance. For example, our English word "happy" has as its root the Latin word *hap* which means "chance" (as in <u>hap</u>hazard, <u>hap</u>penstance). We understand our English word happy to describe a set of favorable circumstances or some good fortune which has come our way much more than a profoundly and deeply understood sense of well-being.

"Fortunate" (or "how fortunate", Anchor Bible) gets at a part of the meaning as well, but too often is associated with good luck. "Blessed", or its derivatives "How blest" or "O the bliss", which the majority of English Bibles use (KJV, RSV, NIV, NEB, NASB) is problematic for the same reasons, and has the additional disad-vantage in that it is an archaic English word. Its meaning is not easy to discern.

Every great Greek New Testament word seems to have an older

Hebrew word standing in its shadow. These Hebrew words inform and subtly shift the meaning of the Greek New Testament words. They fill them with more meaning than these words carry in their own vernacular language. This is true of *markarios* where the Hebrew equivalent is *ashere*. It is this *ashere* which opens the Psalms (1:1) and is scattered throughout the Psalter (32:1). *Ashere* is an exclamation of joy. While our English Bibles try to get at the meaning with words like "blessed", "happy" or "fortunate", it should rightly be translated with the exclamation "O the wonder of it all" or "O the bliss of the person" or another such phrase. It has been noted by Gundry that blessed means "to be congratulated" with more emphasis placed on divine approval than on human happiness. In other words, *markarios* carries with it the sense of ultimate well-being even in the midst of difficulty. *Markarios* transcends our pain, our trials, our failures, and all of our happiness and good luck.

At the center of this word is the unmistakable conviction that God has planted into the Christian's life a wellspring of joy and peace which has the effect of raising the inner spirit to great heights. Blessed does not describe a momentary flash of happiness. It is more than happiness because it is not governed or controlled by circumstances. It is more than being fortunate or having a run of good luck. It is centered in a profound understanding that our life is in the hands of a good God who has given us *markarios* - he has given us bliss.

Jesus promised his embattled followers that a peace quite unlike that which the world gives would be given to them (John 14:27). This peace, joy and sense of well-being begins to get at the rich meaning of *markarios*.

Endurance: facing into the wind. The second part of the beatitude is the virtue that is to be possessed. This virtue is *hupomone* (endurance, perseverance). The present tense reminds us that enduring is a continual process and the active voice suggests we personally must be actively engaged in the enduring.

We have encountered this word before in 1:3. In the earlier usage the emphasis is on enduring the great variety of testings, (*peirasmous*), which come into our lives so completeness and perfection are achieved. Some interpreters (A.T. Robertson, R.P. Martin) suggest that the testing mentioned in verse 12, even though it is the same word as is in verse 2, ought to be rendered "temptations" rather than "testing". In 1:3 the Christian is urged to endure with fortitude while in 1:12 endurance is strengthened to include steadfast resolution. Though both meanings can be derived from *peirasmos*, it seems better to handle both occurrences of the word in a similar fashion. On this basis we are counseled (D. Edmond Hiebert) to translate *peirasmos* consistently with "testing" rather than "temptation" because the text does not caution the Christian to resist the testing but rather to endure it.

Reward: the crown of life. The reward for having faced the wind and having stood tall and firm is that the crown of life is given to the ones who endure. This phrase occurs twice in the New Testament, here in 1:12 and in Revelation 2:10.

The crown of life can be interpreted as a genitive of apposition, meaning it is life itself which is given. To put it positively, the crown is life itself; to put it negatively, the testings of life have the potential to strip the Christian of life. Endurance dismantles the power of death and gives life to the enduring person. It is understood by James that this life comes from God who has given wisdom to those who ask for it so they can endure the most trying trials. This interpretation is consistent with Revelation 2:10 where the crown of life is for those in Smyrna "who have been faithful unto death". The crown of life is for survivors who "remain under" whatever load it is they are asked to carry. The crown of life is for those who face up to life's trials with courage and resolve.

This means we ought not to underestimate the trials which come to us. They are wide-ranging and some have the potential to destroy the believer. Endurance is not needed for the insignificant but troublesome annoyances that come into our lives. Endurance is a virtue because it allows the believing person to come safely through the mine field of trials which have many different degrees of intensity.

The final part of this beatitude, "that God has promised to those who love him," raises two issues which we will encounter again in this epistle. The first concerns the absence of Jesus-language. Earlier we noted (1:5) it is to God we are to address our prayers. We ask God, not Jesus Christ, for the wisdom which helps us solve life's perplexing trials. In this text, which is a summary statement of what has preceded it, it is God again who promises the crown of life to those who successfully endure life's trials. Only twice, once in the opening salutation and the other in the opening injunction prohibiting favoritism is Jesus named.

The second issue, which we will encounter again in 4:5, is that a word from God (or Jesus) is quoted for which we have no reference. Nowhere in either the Old or New Testament is there an explicit statement where God or Jesus promises a crown of life to those who endure. Revelation 2:10 is such a promise but it was written much later than this epistle. Others point to Matthew 19:28 where Jesus promises his disciples they will sit on twelve thrones with him in the new world but that at best is a very oblique reference to the crown of life.

The closest reference to this phrase comes from one of the apocryphal books called <u>The Wisdom of Solomon</u>:

> But the righteous live forever, and their reward is
> with the Lord; the Most High takes care of them.
> Therefore they will receive a glorious crown, and a
> beautiful diadem from the hand of the Lord (5:15-16a).

Some interpreters suggest that many unrecorded sayings of Jesus were kept alive in the oral tradition of the early church (Adamson, Martin). This might well be the case and should not surprise us. Not everything Jesus said has been recorded for our knowing (John 20:31). This saying is well within the realm of believability and is not out of step with the tone of the New Testament. Paul also seems to dip into this oral tradition when he notes "God loves a cheerful giver" (II Cor. 9:7).

Application, Teaching/Preaching Points

This text is rich in meaning both as a summary statement of what has preceded it and as a free-standing text in its own right. Five teaching points arise from this text. All are important to the life of the community of faith.

The reality of the state of "blessedness". Trials by their very nature erode our confidence. Trials have the tendency to undermine the sense that all is well with us. This text flies in the face of such thinking. It asserts that the state of well-being called "blessedness" comes to those who find themselves in the midst of trouble. Too often we consider ourselves "blessed by God" when all is going well. To think of ourselves as being blessed, when in the midst of trials and trauma calls for a new way of thinking and a much more profound understanding of God, the kingdom of God, and the nature of the Christian life. The sign of divine approval is not the absence of trouble, but the receiving of divine wisdom (1:5) so we will be equipped to face with courage and joy the trouble which has come to us.

Endurance helps us stand tall when squeezed by the vice called "trials". We live in a culture that works hard to avoid trouble and trials. We shrink from pain. We are constantly being bombarded with messages that the good life, a life without difficulty, is available to us. While there is no inherent virtue in pain and it is not a sign of spiritual maturity to go looking for it, we also should not go to all extremes to avoid it. We ought not to seek trouble anymore than we try to avoid it. We need both in our lives, and somehow life always finds a way of reminding us of this fact.

The trials which James is writing about are not the kind that go away with a good night's sleep. Unnecessary suffering is foolishness. However, there are some trials that can not be avoided. The Arabs have a proverb which is born in the reality of their environment: "All sunshine makes a desert."

The good things of life have a way of creating a false sense of security within us and often tend to make us lean away from God. Trials, on the other hand, are to push us toward God. Having been driven toward God we can begin to know the rich, well-rounded meaning of *markarios*. The ultimate state of this blessedness is to know we are in the hands of a loving, caring God.

A theology of rewards. There are some things that come to us as a gift from God. Salvation is such a gift. It is given by God and is in effect now. At the end of life we receive eternal life from God which we have now received only as a promise. This is the primary and all-inclusive gift from God; it is his doing. However, this wonderful truth should not lull us to sleep. Our text tells us we have a part in securing one reward which comes from God. It is the crown of life for those survivors who endure. It is for the resolute, the ones who hold faith in all circumstances and stand tall in a time of testing.

The Epistle of James walks a very careful line between that which comes from God and that which comes from us. It attributes to God that which only God can give, and it attributes to the Christian that which is the believing person's responsibility. We will bump into this balance of human and divine responsibility again (2:14-26).

The goodness of God. The topic of the goodness of God is assumed in this section but will be more explicitly stated in 1:16-18. The goodness of God is centered in God's ability to keep promises which are for our security and well-being. The guarantee that God is good and reliable is borne out by the witness of those who have endured. From God they have received blessedness. The blessedness which is the present possession of every persevering believer. Contrary to worldly thinking, joy, peace and well-being can be ours because we have already received life from God. This sense of well-being is a foretaste of the blessedness we will enjoy when the fullness of the crown of life is given to us at the end. (Rev. 2:10).

Loving God is as important as enduring trials. It is not enough to simply grit the teeth and bear whatever comes into our life. In 1:2 James calls the believing person to "Consider it pure joy" when trials come along. In 1:12 the focus is on loving God. This text is not set into a homily on the goodness of life but is about the troublesome trials of life. Therefore, loving God is not a sentimental feeling directed toward the great Giver of wisdom but the clear-headed choice to love in spite of trials and trouble. Love is both a feeling and a choice; sometimes love can exist without feeling but love can never exist without choice. This means the person who knows that "God is love" (I John 4:7ff) also knows that love can be a costly and sacrificial choice. It means that loving God adds to our sense of well-being, our sense of being blessed. Indeed, loving God and seeing him as the One who allows testing to come to us allows us to worship and serve him as a good God. Conversely, being able to sustain our love for God while in the midst of the most pressing trauma and trouble is the ultimate test of whether we belong to God or not.

Personal Response

* Enduring is the ability to stay under the load and carry whatever it is that is your lot to bear. This takes much fortitude. DISCUSS: What is it in your life that requires this kind of discipline? What is the thing which you have to carry to the destination?

* Rewards are mostly given by God and usually come to us as a gift from him. The "crown of life", however, is not a gift as much as it is a reward for enduring. DISCUSS: Why do you think God placed this particular reward into the bevy of rewards that are to come to us? If the immediate meaning of this reward is that we have life here and now, how is this life expressed in your experience?

* Loving God is more a choice than a feeling. We are conditioned to think of love as mostly a feeling. DISCUSS: What are the practical implications of choosing to love? How do the trials of life make this difficult? What are the benefits of loving God in the midst of trials? How is this different from loving God when things are going well for us?

* God's promises are sure. This requires faith, trust and believing. DISCUSS: Is it possible for you to believe God when it seems God has not removed the trials which beset you?

CHAPTER FOUR

Living In A Troubled World:
The Pitfalls Of Self-Deception

When tempted, no one should say, "God is tempting me."
For God cannot be tempted by evil, nor does he tempt any-
one; but each one is tempted when, by his own evil desire, he
is dragged away and enticed. Then, after desire has con-
ceived, it gives birth to sin; and sin, when it is full-grown,
gives birth to death.

Don't be deceived, my dear brothers. Every good and per-
fect gift is from above, coming down from the Father of the
heavenly lights, who does not change like shifting shadows.
He chose to give us birth through the word of truth, that we
might be a kind of firstfruits of all he created.

My dear brothers, take note of this: Everyone should be
quick to listen, slow to speak and slow to become angry, for
man's anger does not bring about the righteous life that God
desires. Therefore, get rid of all moral filth and the evil that
is so prevalent, and humbly accept the word planted in you,
which can save you.

Do not merely listen to the word, and so deceive your-
selves. Do what it says. Anyone who listens to the word but
does not do what it says is like a man who looks at his face in
a mirror and, after looking at himself, goes away and imme-
diately forgets what he looks like. But the man who looks in-
tently into the perfect law that gives freedom, and continues
to do this, not forgetting what he has heard, but doing it —
he will be blessed in what he does.

If anyone considers himself religious and yet does not keep
a tight rein on his tongue, he deceives himself and his religion

*is worthless. Religion that God our Father accepts as pure
and faultless is this: to look after orphans and widows in their
distress and to keep oneself from being polluted by the world
(James 1:13-27).*

The Flow and Form of the Text

The unit is divided into five paragraphs, each dealing with a
separate subject, but all five are tied together in unity. The larger
unit opens with a prohibition against accusing God, "God is
tempting me," and concludes with a clarion call "to keep oneself
from being polluted by the world." The unity of this text is created by two factors: the context of the subject material and the linguistic internal unity. The first factor ties this material to that
which has preceded it. The central word, carried over from the
earlier material, is *peirasmos* (testing). Almost everything which
has preceded this unit has addressed the problem of testings.
James has been very concerned that testings and trials be seen in a
particular way. He has stressed that testings are inevitable and the
believer must endure these trials as a matter of course. James has
asserted that these *peirasmos* are designed to test our endurance
which in turn produces maturity.

The unspoken question which James now anticipates is this: If
it is true that testings come from God, then surely it must also be
God who leads the person into temptation and sinful behaviors.
The opening verse of this unit addresses this matter. But there is
more to this text. In typical flow-of-consciousness fashion, James
allows his fertile mind to explore not only this problem but also
some of the subtle ways in which sinful behavior is expressed in
life, relationships and the community.

The second factor holding this text together is its internal unity.
In pastoral concern for the fledgling church, James issues three
cautions against self-deception. The first caution (1:16) warns
against being deceived about the nature of sin and the character
of God. This is a little problematic grammatically as it can be the
closing sentence of the first paragraph or the opening sentence of
the second paragraph. It also could be a freestanding single-sen-

tence paragraph thereby acting as a caution which influences both the first and second paragraphs. The second caution (1:22) warns against the faulty rationalization that hearing the word of God is enough. Not so, argues James, there must also be a doing of the word. And the third caution (1:26) closely follows the nuance of the second caution; that is, the believer is not to be deceived about what constitutes an appropriate "religious" life. It must, of necessity, involve the practical service dimensions of the Christian life.

The Text Explained

This text is divided into five blocks of material. Each paragraph begins with either a prohibition, a caution or a command, and concludes with a summary statement. Also, each paragraph follows logically in sequence and order.

The nature of sin (vv.13-15) The paragraph opens with a blunt statement that God is not the source of temptation. *Peirasmos* in this case ought to be translated as temptation (Ropes, Dibelius/Greeven) rather than testing as in 1:2,12. This paragraph, reminiscent of the opening line of the epistle, asserts the inevitability of trials and temptation. In 1:2 James writes, "Consider it pure joy whenever you face trials;" in 1:13 he writes, "When tempted." What is not at issue is whether or not the believer faces temptations; rather, the issue is who the source of this temptation might be and what the intended outcome has become. In 1:2ff the author of such testing is unknown and the intent is to foster an endurance which leads to maturity. In 1:13-15 it is explicitly stated that it is not God who is the source of testing and temptation. And the intended outcome of such *peirasmos* is not maturity but the seduction into sin. It is for this reason that almost all of our English Bibles translate *peirasmos* in this text with the word "temptation" rather than "testing".

The believing person ought never to say, "God is tempting me" because of two important facts: God cannot be tempted by evil, nor does God tempt anyone to do evil. The reason for this is the character of God. In the next paragraph James will assert that God is light and "shifting shadows" are not part of his being.

The sources of temptation in this context are the individuals themselves. Strange as it might seem, except for 3:15 and 4:7 where the devil is mentioned, James understands human sinfulness to come from within persons rather than in response to the direct onslaught of the devil. In other words, if following God is a choice, then committing sinful deeds is also a choice. James seems to be emphasizing that no believing person ought to blame someone or some other force for the choices which are made in life, though the mention of the devil in this epistle ought to alert the believer to his existence.

In this text, the process of sinning is a logical sequence of events: persons are tempted by their own evil desires. Two participles, *exelkomenos* (to draw out, to lure away) and *deleazomenos* (to entice or catch by the use of bait) colorfully describe the process of giving in to temptation. Desire is conceived, it gives birth to a sinful act, and the carrying out of sin leads to death.

The character of God (vv.16-18) "Don't be deceived, my dear brothers [and sisters]" is a passionate call to vigilance. This is the first of three exhortations against self-deception. Most English Bibles (NIV, GNB, NEB, JB) make this prohibition and apply it to the opening sentence of the paragraph which deals with the character of God. It can, however, also be the closing sentence of the previous paragraph (NRSV) where the believer is urged not to be deceived about the insidious nature of sin which arises from personal desires. One translation (NASB) makes it stand alone as a paragraph, thereby acting as both a caution against being deceived and a caution against not being deceived about the character of God.

James begins his treatment of the character of God by developing what he alluded to in the first paragraph of this passage. Earlier he argued that God cannot be tempted by evil, nor does he tempt anyone to do evil. Now James takes this a step farther. Not only is God immune to evil and incapable of tempting anyone with evil, but all the gifts he gives are good and perfect and flow out of his character. God who is good and in whom there is no evil gives good (*agathos*) gifts. They are good precisely because God is good. *Agathos* can also be translated "kind, benevolent, wholesome, beneficial, dependable" (Gingrich, p. 1-2). All of these words describe

God as well; therefore God only gives gifts which are compatible with his character. Further, these good gifts have a consistency to them because they come from the God who never changes. God, who is light and the creator of the heavenly lights, cannot cause darkness and cannot give gifts which represent the forces of darkness. All of his gifts have the unmistakable brightness of having come from "the Father of heavenly lights".

James concludes this paragraph by highlighting the ultimate gift, the gift of new birth. In the earlier paragraph, the life-cycle process of conception, birth and death was used to describe the pattern of sin. In this sentence, birth is effected by the word of truth. God is a God of direct, deliberate action. What he does, he does intentionally. The act of choosing "to give to us birth", (1:18) is as deliberate as a pregnant woman giving birth to a child. This birth leads to a life which is described as "firstfruits". This recalls the Old Testament Feast of Firstfruits (Lev. 23:9-14) where, in anticipation of the abundance of harvest, the first sheaves of grain were brought to God in a celebration of thanksgiving.

On listening, speaking and controlling anger (vv.19-21) James, the consummate pastor, is more interested in how the believer's faith applies to life than in setting out a reasoned theological perspective on the subject. As usual, by setting out the ethical boundaries of an issue, James unintentionally sets out a theological rationale for such a position.

Earlier, in the middle of an extended treatment on trials, endurance and maturity (1:9-11) he came out swinging against the favored treatment of the rich, which he will address again in 2:1-13. In this text, in the middle of his discourse on the nature of God and the nature of sin, he addresses the matter of listening, speaking and anger.

"My dear brothers," a formula James uses twelve times, usually introduces an ethical appeal. The appeal has three parts: "quick to listen, slow to speak and slow to become angry." These three exhortations have the wit and style of a proverb (Prov. 10:19; 14:29; 17:28) and recall the words of Jesus: "Out of the abundance of the heart the mouth speaks. By your words, you shall be condemned or set free" (Matt. 12:34,37).

This threefold ethical injunction concerns the tongue; when not to speak, when to speak and how to speak. James has an inordinate preoccupation with the problems caused by improper speech. He will return to the topic again and again (1:26; 2:16-17; 3:1-12; 4:1-3; 5:9,12). Being immersed in the Hebrew wisdom tradition, James cautions the fledgling church that it is always safer to have careful speech and few words than too much speaking. It is always better to be known for listening than for speaking. Much speaking leads to sin, the sages of Israel argued (Prov. 10:19). Much speaking leads to disputes and disputes lead to angry words, and an angry outburst "does not bring about the righteous life that God desires." Righteous in this context refers not to the righteousness that is part of God's character but to the way of life appropriate to a believing person (Rienecker, Adamson).

The final sentence of this paragraph, "get rid of all moral filth and the evil that is so prevalent," seems to indicate there is more than merely angry words. The sins which James mentions seem to be the sins which are common to all generations of Christians. They are the sins of favoritism, quarreling, piling up riches for security, the arrogance in thinking that all of life is in our own hands and mistreating employees. These are more than just the sins of speaking and anger. If these are the sins which refer to the "moral filth and the evil that is so prevalent," then James paints the common sins of the church in the most vivid colors possible.

The answer to such sins, as is the answer to the nature of sin, is "the word". In this context, the word is "planted in you" and "can save you".

The problem of intentional self-deception (vv. 22-25) There is nothing as devastating to the human spirit as to live with self-deception. To be deceived about a matter is one thing; to live with intentional self-deception is quite another issue. Sometimes we are deceived inadvertently. We are misinformed and we make judgments which are inappropriate. Good intentions and sincerity do little to make our miscalculations less wrong, but at least we can assert we were sincerely wrong. Self-deception, on the other hand, is the deliberate denial of reality. It is the intentional act of believing something that is false. The great tragedy of self-deception is that we deliberately distort the truth to make it more acceptable to us.

The answer to having been deceived inadvertently is to change our minds when the truth comes to light. It is more difficult with willful self-deception. Since willful self-deception has distorted truth to make it more palatable, a thorough change within the inner being is needed so truth and reality will prevail.

This fourth paragraph addresses the problem of intentional self-deception. This is practiced in the reading or hearing of the word of truth and not acting on it. This, James suggests, is like looking in a mirror, seeing our reflection and walking away, thinking we are different than what we actually saw in the mirror.

The antidote to self-deception, the nature of human sinfulness and its implications, (1:15,18) and the problem of "moral filth and the evil which is so prevalent" (1:21) is again the word of truth, this time called "the perfect law that gives freedom" (1:25). The answer to self-deception lies in a continual looking into the law of freedom, and "not forgetting ... but doing it." To a large degree, James argues, our personal spiritual vitality and health is in our own hands.

The concluding clause, "he will be blessed in what he does," recalls the thrust of the beatitude just announced (1:12). There will be a sense of inner well-being, a calmness of peace within those who read, hear, understand and act!

Worthless and faultless religion (vv. 26-27) The third and final warning concerning self-deception involves how God sees our lives. James draws on the eighth century prophets, particularly Micah 6:8, and sets out the requirements of true religion in both negative and positive terms. The negative characteristics are to be avoided; the positive qualities are to be practiced.

Worthless religion is noisy religion where there is endless talking, probably about faith and those things which tend to cause anger. The phrase, "yet does not keep a tight rein on his tongue," indicates that a loose tongue is causing problems within the community of faith. James once again draws on Hebrew wisdom literature where David the Psalmist counsels "Do not be like the horse or the mule, which have no understanding but must be controlled by bit and bridle or they will not come to you" (Ps. 32:9).

This illustrates how firmly the people of God must control speech. Worthless religion is uncontrolled, undisciplined speech without corresponding actions.

The theme of religious talk, even proper faith-talk without subsequent action, will surface again in this brief epistle, much more powerfully in the faith-works section (2:14-26).

Positive religion that pleases God is active religion. "Pure and faultless religion" has three characteristics: it tends the orphans, takes notice of the widow's distress and does something about it, and is proactive in keeping oneself unpolluted by the values and norms of society.

Application, Teaching/Preaching Points

This text is a rich source for teaching in the church and addresses many points which are often overlooked in the lives of believers. Three main points deserve comment.

The nature of sin. Though not denying the presence and influence of the devil, James puts the emphasis for responsibility of sinful behavior on the individual. This is in keeping with his understanding of the Christian life. We have the freedom to choose, therefore we are accountable for the choices we make. It is part of our fallenness that we want to blame someone else for our actions (Gen. 3:11-13).

In this text, blame for sinful behaviors is wrongfully assigned to God. The unspoken charge is that God is the one who tempts the believer with evil. In our day the emphasis seems to have shifted to the devil who is seen to be the source of all practiced evil. While this is partially correct, it is not the whole story. Without belittling the influence or deceptive effect of the devil, many of the temptations persons experience simply come from within themselves. Sin blossoms when desire arises within and sin incubates within us when we like what we see or think. Sin takes root when we mull on it, enjoying its tantalizing grip on our minds. It becomes an action when we play out this fantasy in our life. The human penchant for blaming someone other than oneself for sinful behavior makes a mockery of grace which absolves the believer of sins, both intentional and inadvertent.

Sin is present in all of humanity and is a part of every Christian's experience. Sinful thoughts and actions arise deep within our being. Recognizing where this sin has its origins does not make it any less sinful, but it does allow us to bring every thought into captivity (II Cor. 10:5) and accept accountability for every part of our life.

The character of God. The character of God as we have come to understand him is determined by how the Scriptures have revealed him to us. What we know about God is what God has intended us to know about him. Since God is greater than his self-revelation to humanity and the Scriptures can not describe all he is, we tend to create portraits of God which are compatible with our notions of what he should be and how he ought to behave.

The Scriptures are clear about the character of God. Although the biblical portrait is as complex as God himself, there is a remarkable consistency in the way God is portrayed in the Bible. This portrait ties together a God who is both merciful and just, hidden and revealed, Savior and Judge. The human desire for taking one image of God and making it the dominant image at the expense of the varied nature and character of God means we can create an image of God that is to our liking and which serves our purposes.

James was writing to the scattered church which had particular views of God. Some apparently saw God as tempter and tester. Without wanting to present a theological treatise, James nonetheless presents a brief but complete picture of God First, God is the generous giver of wisdom (1:5), a wisdom that comes from above (3:17); God is a rewarder of those who endure to the end (1:12, 5:7-11); God is just and exercises his sovereign will in choosing the poor over the rich (2:5) and is not impressed with those who speak of faith without putting it into action (1:26-27, 2:14-26); God is judge (4:12); and finally, God hears the fervent prayers of humanity (5:13-18).

The teaching and application of this varied portrait of God will guarantee that personal agendas will not dominate the community of faith.

The danger of self-deception. It has been wisely noted that the only two things for which there are no antidotes are self-righteousness and self-deception. Both are terminal diseases. Self-deception is rooted in a false understanding of reality and a virtual denial of reality.

In the fairytale *Snow White and the Seven Dwarfs,* the wicked witch fully expected to have her vanity confirmed when she cried, "Mirror, mirror on the wall, who is the fairest of them all?" Self-deception expresses itself in both the questions we ask and the answers we expect to receive. When the expected answer is different from what we receive, it creates much anxiety.

The church must constantly be vigilant against the insidious influence of living with false portraits about the nature of sin, the character of God, , and a partnership between confession and good deeds.

Personal Response

* God's goodness is reflected in his acts. God's gifts, therefore, are good as well. It is always easier to confess a great truth than live by its guiding power. DISCUSS: If God is good and all his gifts to us are good, how do we reconcile his will to give us freedom of choice, which grants us the right to succumb to temptation to sin?

* James, while not denying the power of the devil, places the responsibility for our sinfulness on humanity itself. There is something powerfully natural about how sin is conceived, born and practiced. A few decades ago a comedian popularized the phrase, "The devil made me do it." DISCUSS: Look at the passage and at your own experience to see if James is correct in placing responsibility for sin on humanity itself. Can you think of a situation where sin is born without the conscious choice of the person involved?

* Self-deception is a very devastating thing. It is one thing to be wrong about a matter. It is, however, very different with self-deception. DISCUSS: Why is James so adamant that we ought not to be deceived about the nature of God? Why does James want us to be deceived about the nature of sin? How can we ensure that we will not fall victim to self-deception? Why is it so hard to come

to the truth about a matter when we practice self-deception?

* Godly living is demonstrated more by the actions we do than the beliefs we verbalize. DISCUSS: Is it "overkill" when James calls religion worthless if it does not have a social conscience? In our society, the plight of the widow and orphan is largely handled by government agencies. Is there still a role for the church and individual believers to do good for the lonely, the destitute and the hard-pressed?

CHAPTER FIVE

Dancing To A Different Drumbeat:
On Snobbery And Favoritism

My brothers, as believers in our glorious Lord Jesus Christ, don't show favoritism. Suppose a man comes into your meeting wearing a gold ring and fine clothes, and a poor man in shabby clothes also comes in. If you show special attention to the man wearing fine clothes and say, "Here's a good seat for you," but say to the poor man, "You stand there" or "Sit here on the floor by my feet," have you not discriminated among yourselves and become judges with evil thoughts?

Listen, my dear brothers: Has not God chosen those who are poor in the eyes of the world to be rich in faith and to inherit the kingdom he promised those who love him? But you have insulted the poor. Is it not the rich who are exploiting you? Are they not the ones who are dragging you into court? Are they not the ones who are slandering the noble name of him to whom you belong?

If you really keep the royal law found in Scripture, "Love your neighbor as yourself," you are doing right. But if you show favoritism, you sin and are convicted by the law as lawbreakers. For whoever keeps the whole law and yet stumbles at just one point is guilty of breaking all of it. For he who said, "Do not commit adultery," also said, "Do not murder." If you do not commit adultery but do commit murder, you have become a lawbreaker.

Speak and act as those who are going to be judged by the law that gives freedom, because judgment without mercy will be shown to anyone who has not been merciful. Mercy triumphs over judgment! (James 2:1-13)

The Flow and Form of the Text

These four paragraphs have stronger content unity than anything we have encountered so far. Gone is the free flow of ideas
where one idea leads to another. This text is tightly written. James
introduces the subject of snobbery and favoritism with an appeal
in the name of "our glorious Lord Jesus Christ", the second of only
two references to Jesus Christ in the whole epistle, and then he develops the theme with remarkable discipline.

The writing tools he uses to make his case are fourfold: first, he
introduces the topic of favoritism and snobbery with a hypothetical situation. As with all good illustrative material, this story has
roots in the reality of first century culture. Second, he appeals to
the scattered church's personal experiences with the rich to add
weight to the hypothetical story. This personal experience serves
to deepen the sense of injustice which the story has highlighted.
Third, James calls to remembrance that which every devout Hebrew would know by rote - the "royal law" or "the law that gives
freedom" which he introduced to his readers in 1:25. And fourth,
James reinterprets the Old Testament law by giving it the distinct
flavor which Jesus himself added in the Sermon on the Mount.

The progression of thought from the opening line is connected
to and flows from the concluding sentence of the earlier pericope.
True religion, James has argued, is religion that takes note of the
distress of the disadvantaged and reaches out to help. All religious claims expressed only in words are bogus claims. In this
passage this principle statement is put to the test in a very practical manner.

The unspoken question which this text asks is: Can the scattered
church live by the new reality and understanding that all persons
are equal and have the right to equal dignity in the community of
faith? Or will the church simply mirror the existing cultural values
and reject the new ethic, the ethic of Jesus himself on whose behalf
this appeal is being made (2:1). The answer must be a resounding
"yes". If not, the claims of Christianity are compromised. As evidence that a new beginning has been made and it is possible to live
with the New Kingdom reality, James closes this section with a triumphant shout, "Mercy triumphs over judgment!"

Each of the four paragraphs have three distinct internal points giving the structure almost a poetic flavor. These four triads always begin with a declaration of fact, then move into a statement of reality and conclude with a judgment statement.

The Text Explained

A hypothetical story (vv. 1-4) The first paragraph begins with a strong prohibition against favoritism. The force of the prohibition is strengthened through the use of the present tense which suggests this prohibition is always in force. The imperative mood makes it a command, and the use of the clause "as believers in our glorious Lord Jesus Christ" adds weight to the command. In other words, this is not simply the opinion of James the writer; it is spoken on behalf of Jesus himself.

The hypothetical story takes only one sentence to tell. The rich man is identified by the telltale signs of importance and wealth, a gold ring and fine clothes. It was common in both Roman and Jewish society for the rich to wear many rings (Mayor). Often the rich would wear white linen togas whitened to a glistening state with chalk (Rienecker). The poor man in this story is readily identified by his shabby clothes. Poor (*ptochos*) is a very strong word describing those who are abjectly, grindingly, beggarly poor. The contrast established by James is overwhelming. The rich man is rich to the point of ostentation; the poor man is poor to the point of not having enough to survive. In no way, using normative cultural standards, are these men equals.

The third and clinching sentence, a rhetorical question, sets up the case study in dramatic terms. The negative *ou diekrithate* expects a "yes" answer to the question. In other words, saying to the rich, "Here is a good seat" and to the poor, "You stand there" or "Sit here on the floor by my feet", means that a serious breach in the equality of all persons under God has been perpetrated. *Diekrithate* can be translated many ways: to judge between two, to face both ways, to be divided among oneself, to waiver or to distinguish between. In this context it is probably best to translate this "to distinguish between".

Though it is not explicitly stated, it appears that both the rich

man and the poor man are members of the church. So this discrimination is not an attempt to make a stranger feel comfortable
in the gathered meeting. The inclusion of "among yourselves"
probably means this distinction was arrived at by the common
consensus of the group.

The oppressive reputation of the rich (vv. 5-7) The second
paragraph again is characterized by a triad. It begins with a question in which the negative *oux ho theos* assumes a positive answer.
This question has the force of an exclamatory sentence; it could be
translated, "Of course we know that God has chosen the poor to
be rich in faith and to inherit the kingdom!"

In the Sermon on the Mount, Jesus declared "the kingdom of
heaven" to be granted to the ones who are "poor in spirit" (Matt.
5:3). In the Sermon on the Plain, this same saying is simplified by
Luke, "Blessed are you who are poor, for yours is the kingdom of
God" (Luke 6:20). In a parable told by Jesus, the rich Pharisee is
denied entry into the kingdom of God while the beggarly poor
Lazarus is granted entry (Luke 16:19-31).

We must be careful to guard against a simplistic reading of this
paragraph. The issue is not a matter of those who are poor in material goods having gained entry into the kingdom of God, while
those who are rich being automatically damned to eternal perdition. James chooses his words very carefully. To be "poor in the
eyes of the world" and "to be rich in faith and to inherit the kingdom" speaks about an inner life of faith and an attitude, as well as
a person's station in life. For James, faith gives entry into the in-
heritance of the kingdom, and faith, when it is merged with humility, leads to vast riches.

The second part of this triad is the blunt assertion, "You have
insulted *hetimasate:* literally dishonored the poor." The insult is
created when we accept the idea that to be rich and important
makes a person more acceptable in the eyes of God than to be poor
and destitute. The presence or absence of wealth has nothing to
do with how God measures a person. We insult the poor if we
think God looks at them with disdain, the same way society looks
down at them. The writer of Proverbs puts it well: "He who
mocks the poor shows contempt for their Maker" (17:5). We also

insult the poor when we assume that poverty with respect to material possessions grants automatic entry into the kingdom.

The third part of this paragraph strings together three rhetorical questions to which the answer must always be a resounding "Yes, of course they do!" Three strong words are used to describe the actions of the rich. First, they oppress (*kataunasteuousin*) the poor. Some translations strengthen this verb by translating it "exploit" (NIV). Not only do they oppress the poor but they do it constantly (present tense) and intentionally (active voice). Second, they drag (*elkousin*) the poor into the courts where they will be at a distinct disadvantage. Again, the present tense and active voice indicate these acts happen all the time and are quite intentional. And third, they blaspheme (*blasphamousin*) the Lord of the church.

The portrait of the rich is not very complimentary. The rich are seen as oppressive, powerful, and without regard or respect for God. All that matters is the accumulation of wealth. The rich are portrayed as willing to go to any lengths, even to slandering "the noble name" of God.

The demands of the royal law (vv. 8-11) The third paragraph of this discreet unit puts us in touch with one of the central themes of the epistle. In 1:23-24, James has argued that to listen to the word and not act on it is as futile as looking into a mirror and promptly forgetting what one has seen. On the other hand, if a person acts on what has been heard, "he will be blessed in all he does." In 1:26-27 James strengthens his argument by asserting that the willful neglect of acting on what has been heard is to deceive oneself and to practice worthless religion.

James applies this same principle to the relationships between the rich and the poor by creating a logical sequence of thought. The paragraph opens with a statement of fact; it then moves on to apply this principle statement to the matter of the rich and the poor in the church; and finally, James sets the principle into the larger context of what sinful behavior truly is.

The statement of fact in 2:8 simply asserts that the royal law, "Love your neighbor as yourself," is not to be ignored. It is a first-class conditional phrase which means it is assumed to be true and is not open for debate. This royal law is a foundation in all human relationships which are to be governed by it. The royal law, as cited in the Old Testament (Lev.19:18) is carried over into this text almost word for word.

When asked by the Sadducees and Pharisees what was the greatest commandment (Matt. 22:34-40), Jesus takes two Old Testament texts and ties them together: "Love the Lord your God with all your heart and with all your soul and with all your strength" (Deut. 6:5) and "Love your neighbor as yourself" (Lev. 19:18). And then he added, "All the Law and the Prophets hang on these two commandments." Not only did Jesus understand that these two elements belong together, so did the lawyer who asked Jesus how he might receive eternal life (Luke 10:25ff).

Strange as it might seem, James quotes only the first half of this famous diptych, "Love your neighbor as yourself." The context determines the subject is human relationships in the community of faith, not the personal relationship with God. The power of this statement is remarkable. In simple, easy-to-understand language, James sets out the demands of the royal law: "If you really keep the royal law found in Scripture, 'Love your neighbor as yourself,' you are doing right."

The second stage to the logical progression of thought in this paragraph asks the "So what?" question. What does it mean to keep the royal law? Negatively stated, if favoritism is shown, sin is committed because this law is not being kept. And if sin is committed in this matter, then "you .. are convicted by the law as lawbreakers".

This is a harsh statement and reflects James' immersion in Old Testament thinking where great emphasis is placed on proper relationships. The property laws, the laws governing civic duties and behaviors, the laws governing moral behaviors, and the consequences of illicit and criminal behavior all put the emphasis on civil order and the protection of the weak. The Old Testament law was given to establish a society in which the dignity of each person was to be protected. Leviticus 18-19 is particularly instructive where God adds more than a dozen times, "I am the Lord your God" to add weight to the laws which govern interpersonal relationships.

When Micah summed up the demands of the law, he cried out, "What does the Lord require of you, O man? To act justly, to love mercy and to walk humbly before your God" (6:8). James in his role as church statesman and pastor, cries out, "And what does God demand from you? To love your neighbor as yourself, and to not show favoritism to the rich and the powerful!"

The New Testament strengthens this emphasis. In Christ, all the barriers which society has put in place to protect the rights of the privileged class have come down. In Christ there is no male or female, no slave or free, no Jew or Greek (Gal. 3:28).

The third part of this paragraph highlights the nature and character of sin. An all-embracing statement is given and then, to drive the point home, an illustration is provided. In keeping with the high demands of the law, James sets out the pervasive and unforgiving nature of sin. The intent of this statement, "For whoever keeps the whole law and yet stumbles at just one point is guilty of breaking it all" is to issue a strong caution against selective obedience. James is not saying that "to stumble at just one point" means we have violated and broken all of the law (Hiebert), nor does it mean the stumbling person is guilty of every serious breach listed in the law. To be guilty (*enochos*) literally means to be in the power of evil which cannot keep from breaking the law.

In the illustration, James chooses his words very carefully. "For he who said, 'Do not commit adultery,' also said, 'Do not commit murder.' If you do not commit adultery but do commit murder, you have become a lawbreaker." James is not comparing favoritism with committing adultery or murder. In the normal scheme of things and certainly in terms of societal values and viewpoints, favoritism is a lesser sin. The point of the illustration is to focus attention on a holy God and the standard he demands. A person cannot willfully despise another human being and be pleasing to God anymore than he can violate another commandment and remain in God's favor (Harper).

Pastoral counsel (vv. 12-13) The three-part counsel is blunt and to the point. First, the encouragement is to live with an eye toward the law which gives freedom. If you treat every person with respect and avoid the pitfalls of snobbery and favoritism, you will be free from the law which has the power to condemn you in the present and judge you in the future.

Second, a warning is issued concerning the nature of judgment. The measuring stick we use to judge others will be used by God in measuring us. This echoes the words of Jesus who spoke repeatedly on this subject. The One who said, "Blessed are the merciful, for they shall receive mercy" (Matt. 5:7) also warned in the Lord's Prayer, " If you forgive men when they sin against you, your heavenly Father will also forgive you. But if you do not forgive men their sins, your Father will not forgive your sins" (Matt. 6:14-15). In a parable spoken in response to a query by Peter about how many times he ought to forgive his brother, Jesus reminded his disciples that forgiveness once given can be invalidated if we do not also extend forgiveness to others (Matt. 18:21-35). James is very clear and passionate: "Judgment without mercy will be shown to anyone who has not been merciful."

And third, this pericope ends with a triumphant shout of victory: "Mercy triumphs over judgment!" Forgiveness is stronger than hate. Showing mercy is the sign that the kingdom of God has come and is present on earth. Equality of personhood in the community of faith is always more uplifting than maintaining the carefully protected privileges of the rich and famous. Mercy and forgiveness break down the walls which separate one human being from another.

Application, Teaching/Preaching Points

This is an explosive text. In our culture, as in the early Roman-Greco world, there are many societal divisions which are carried over into the church. Three points deserve comment.

Dismantling favoritism. There is a fine line between showing favoritism and showing respect. Great care must be exercised in applying this text to current church life. There are common courtesies which simply reflect decency. Showing respect is a fine Christian virtue and ought to be encouraged. Good manners, when addressing either the rich or the poor, must not be interpreted as favoritism. Nor is it favoritism when, in the presence of outstanding women or men, respect and courtesy are shown. The

Scriptures are full of exhortations to honor the king (I Peter 2:17), to submit to those in authority (Rom. 13:1ff), to pray for those who govern (I Tim. 2:1ff), and to hold in respect the congregational leaders of the church (Heb. 13:7). We do well to heed this biblical counsel.

This text confronts what happens within the community of faith. In our culture, wealth and power go together and we tend to stand in awe of greatness. Greatness is acknowledged when someone accomplishes extraordinary things which are usually beyond our reach. This text calls the church to stand against our natural inclinations by not allowing these extraordinary persons to claim special preferential treatment.

In the hypothetical story James tells, the rich are stereotyped as evil people. They are the ones who prey on the poor. And God knows there are enough of these kinds of people everywhere. Adamson reminds us that not every rich man is doomed to eternal perdition and not every poor person is sure to be saved. James contrasts the worst of the rich with the best of the poor. Care must be taken not to lump all people into stereotypical classes, thereby violating the grace of God in all persons' lives.

Not only are we to guard against favoritism, we are to dismantle it so thoroughly that it has no place to gain a foothold. James warns against allowing ourselves to even think discriminating thoughts.

Doing what is right is the ultimate test of our faith. Quite simply, Christianity is loving our neighbor as ourselves. If it is true that love covers a multitude of sins (I Peter 4:8b) then loving our neighbors and serving their interests with the same degree of urgency that we use to serve our own will make faith come alive in our communities. Conversely, not loving our neighbor, and we do this by discriminating against the ones who are different from us, is tantamount to dismantling our own faith. An old proverb says it well: "The proof of the pudding is in the eating!"

Payday is coming. Judgment is not something we discuss very often in the church. The church tends to be quite comfortable with the understanding that those who reject the faith will be judged at the end of history. However, this passage is not directed against the ungodly; rather, it affirms judgment is also to be exercised within the community of faith.

This is the first of many warnings in this epistle that judgment is a reality. For James, judgment is always reserved for the ones who know what is required but intentionally fail to measure up to the demands of the faith-life. In an ironic, surprising twist in thinking, James argues there is a judgment reserved for the ones who willfully discriminate against the poor. The measuring guide in judgment is, curiously enough, the same one used against the poor. In a strange manner of thinking, judgment is tit-for-tat.

Personal Response

* God is active in the world creating a new people for himself. This "new people" is to reflect the values and realities of Christ. The great danger for the church is to be so mesmerized by the values and norms of society that it begins to reflect the culture more than its newness. DISCUSS: How far must the church go in reflecting the new reality that in Christ there is no distinction between the rich and poor, educated and uneducated, male and female? What practical steps are necessary to ensure these new standards are practiced in the church?

* Every local congregation is comprised of people from varying backgrounds, differing vocations, wide-ranging interests and wealth. Together these people comprise the oneness of the church. It also creates stresses within the body of Christ. DISCUSS: Some people have opined that churches ought to be structured along homogeneous lines; that is, the local congregation ought to have mainly people with the same interests, backgrounds and wealth in it. What do you think?

* Jesus affirmed the lawyer's answer when he agreed that the greatest of all commandments is "to love the Lord your God" and "to love your neighbor as yourself". This saying of Jesus, which James repeats in the second part of this passage, has sometimes been interpreted to mean we ought to love ourselves, because without self-love we cannot love our neighbor. DISCUSS: What do you think about this way of interpreting 2:8?

* James makes the point that if we keep the whole law but

stumble in only one point, we are guilty of breaking the whole law (2:10). DISCUSS: How do you see this matter? Does the fact that we all sin mean there is no value in keeping the moral laws of God?

CHAPTER SIX

Living With Wholesome Tension: Faith And Works

What good is it, my brothers, if a man claims to have faith but has no deeds? Can such faith save him? Suppose a brother or sister is without clothes and daily food. If one of you says to him, "Go, I wish you well; keep warm and well fed," but does nothing about his physical needs, what good is it? In the same way, faith by itself, if it is not accompanied by action, is dead.

But someone will say, "You have faith; I have deeds."

Show me your faith without deeds, and I will show you my faith by what I do. You believe that there is one God. Good! Even the demons believe that — and shudder.

You foolish man, do you want evidence that faith without deeds is useless? Was not our ancestor Abraham considered righteous for what he did when he offered his son Isaac on the altar? You see that his faith and his actions were working together, and his faith was made complete by what he did. And the Scripture was fulfilled that says, "Abraham believed God, and it was credited to him as righteousness," and he was called God's friend. You see that a person is justified by what he does and not by faith alone.

In the same way, was not even Rahab the prostitute considered righteous for what she did when she gave lodging to the spies and sent them off in a different direction? As the body without the spirit is dead, so faith without deeds is dead (James 2:14-26).

The Flow and Form of the Text

It almost seems natural that these thirteen verses should follow on the heels of what has just been written. This passage of Scripture is the final step in the direction James has been pointing the reader since about the middle of the first chapter. The methodology used to develop this theme is question and answer. The unit begins with a rhetorical question which ties the text grammatically to that which has preceded it. Incidentally, this is the sixth such rhetorical question in the chapter and there are four more to come, giving this larger unit remarkable stylistic unity.

The unity of this passage lies both in the form of the text as well as in the content. The text opens with a question, "What good is it, my brothers [and sisters]" and ends with a definitive answer to that question, "As the body without the spirit is dead, so faith without deeds is dead." The four internal questions are simply a question and answer mechanism to bring us around to the desired answer, an answer which brings faith and action together. Five times in this passage James will make essentially the same statement: "faith by itself, if not accompanied by action, is dead" (2:17); "Show me your faith without deeds, and I will show you my faith by what I do" (2:18b); "his faith and his actions were working together, and his faith was made complete by what he did" (2:22); "You see that a person is justified by what he does and not by faith alone" (2:24); and "so faith without deeds is dead" (2:26b).

The Text Explained

The controversy. There is probably no other more highly contested New Testament pericope than this text. The controversy does not lie in the meaning of the words. The central premise is easy enough to understand. The main thrust of this text is that faith must result in a life characterized by good works, which is not controversial at all. The controversy comes when James insists that if there is an absence of good deeds in the life of the believer, there must also be an absence of the faith which saves, because the believer " is justified by what he does and not by faith alone."

This might not be controversial, since it makes sense to most believers that faith and good deeds are inseparable from each other, except that Paul the Apostle makes precisely the opposite point in Romans 4:1-25, using exactly the same illustrative material which James uses.

At first glance it appears that Paul and James are on opposite sides of this dispute, and usually these two passages (James 2:14-26 and Romans 3-5) are set against each other. However, the two writers ask different questions. For Paul the question is: is a person saved by works or by faith? His answer is firm: by faith alone. For James the question is different: what happens if a person claims to have faith but the life is barren of good works? His answer is also firm: if a person claims to have faith, it ought to be demonstrated by a life of good deeds, because faith without good deeds cannot save.

Paul uses the life and experience of Abraham to point out that it was not his good deeds and obedience which saved him; rather, it was that he "believed" and this "belief/faith" was credited to him as righteousness (Rom. 4:1-25). James, using precisely the same material, argues that Abraham had faith and this faith was illustrated when he obediently followed the word and command of God to sacrifice his son Isaac. In other words, had Abraham not followed the instructions of God he would have demonstrated that faith had not been born in his life.

The form which gives structure to this text involves six steps: a provocative, stimulating two-part question is framed; a hypothetical but realistic situation is cited; an initial answer is stated; a protest is anticipated and articulated, and a remarkably caustic answer is hurled back at the protester; two Old Testament illustrations are presented; and the final concluding statement is spoken.

The provocative question. The way this two-part question is framed anticipates a twofold negative answer. "What good is it?" requires a strong negative response: nothing! "Can such faith save him?" also requires a firm negative response: no, of course not! With these two questions the central issue is placed on the table. James serves notice that no listener or reader of this text ought to miss the central point which he is intent on making.

A hypothetical situation. This draws on a common scenario acted out daily in the ancient Near East. Beggars abounded everywhere. Jesus repeatedly met the poor, the blind, the lame, the beggars. In this hypothetical story, a brother or sister is in serious want for the necessities of life. However, rather than filling that need, the person to whom the request has come simply offers a word of peace: "Go, I wish you well; keep warm and keep well fed."

Please note that the hypothetical story ends with a repetition of the question which opened this section: "What good is it?" Again the answer must be a towering "Nothing! Nothing at all!".

The first summary. The summary statement (2:17) is almost redundant at this point, serving only to drive home the same point which the two negative answers have already provided.

A protest is anticipated. James anticipates a retort. The protest does not address the central issue that faith must have deeds to authenticate it. Rather, the protesting person argues it is enough to have either one or the other (2:18). The protester seems convinced that if a person has either faith or deeds, everything will be well. The attitude seems to be that each person should live life as they are inclined to live it, you doing what you are comfortable doing and I doing what I am comfortable doing. So let it lie in peace.

James will have none of this. Belief and good deeds must go together. They are inseparable. To pull them apart is to pronounce death on both faith and good deeds. It simply is not enough to believe, nor is it enough to have only good deeds. And to drive the point home, James sarcastically notes that even the demons believe (2:19). If belief were enough, then surely the demons would also be saved because they believe. But demons, by their very existence, disturb the good that God would do and are thus opposed to God. Therefore belief alone is not enough.

Two illustrations: Abraham and Rahab. The opening vocative, "You foolish man [person]," (2:20) continues the sarcastic assault which the caustic comment about demons has initiated. "Foolish" is spoken in the sense of a person not wanting to accept what is obvious, instead of a demeaning description of someone who can not grasp a concept.

The opening question, "do you want evidence that faith without deeds is useless?" immediately tells us not only the intent of the two illustrations, but also how the material will be used. Concerning Abraham, James' unique twist is the assumption "that his faith and his actions were working together" and in this unique partnership "his faith was made complete by what he did" (2:22).

James is saying that if you can not see the connection between these two issues, then you are "foolish". If a person can not comprehend how these can never be separated, then a person does not have eyes to see spiritual reality. Therefore, when the Old Testament Scriptures say, "Abraham believed God and it was credited to him for righteousness" (Gen. 15:6) God was giving his approval not only to what Abraham believed, but also how he lived and what he did to authenticate that belief.

The second illustration concerns Rahab the prostitute. The Old Testament narrative is rather extensive (Josh. 2:1-24; 6:22-25) and she is listed in Matthew's genealogy (1:5) and the Hebrews list of heroes (11:31). Rahab and her family were the only inhabitants to escape the total devastation of the city of Jericho. The key to her salvation was the deeds of kindness and courage which presented the city of Jericho into the hands of the Israelites. Even the lie she told to protect the presence of the spies hidden on the rooftop was seen as part of her good deeds.

A final concluding statement. The words "As the body without the spirit is dead, so faith without deeds is dead" (2:26) sum up the whole argument of this passage. To argue, as many do, that James and Paul are at each other's throats on this subject is to make too much of the different questions they pose. With Paul the church affirms salvation is by faith and not works; with James the church affirms that faith is demonstrated and completed by a life of good deeds.

Application, Teaching/Preaching Points

This text offers great incentive to the church to be active in a life of good deeds. Good deeds and faith belong together. Rather than endlessly debating the question of salvation by faith (Paul) or a saved life full of good deeds (James), it may be better to focus attention on a life which is lived richly and generously under God. Here are some practical points to think about.

Faith and good deeds complement each other. Jesus mentioned two great statements to his followers: the Great Commandment (Luke 10:27) in which he calls Christians to love their neighbors as themselves, and the Great Commission (Matt. 28:19-20) in which he calls the scattered people of God to be active in making disciples of all nations. These are complementary and belong together. Too often they are separated, not because they are unlinked but because we think we have to put everything in a list of priorities. If we can give our energies to only one thing, we argue, what do I want to give my life to? The evangelical church has usually answered with the priority of evangelism and discipleship. To tend to the soul is seen to be a higher priority than educating people, doing medical work, building homes, initiating development projects and distributing food aid.

However, these two statements of Jesus belong together and should not be separated. What the church and the world need is not less of one and more of the other, but more of both. Faith and good deeds belong together.

On establishing and keeping priorities. Years ago a famous American football coach spoke about the priorities in his life: "God, family and football, in that order." We all identify with the need to establish certain things as being more important than others; however, nothing is quite that easy. On one side of the issue, we serve God by being good family members; we also serve God by being diligent and productive in our chosen careers. Somehow God is to be all mixed into the balance of things which comprise our lives.

On the other side, if we do not say that some things are more important than others, we are damned to treating everything which comes into our lives as being equal. This sends us scurrying in so many directions that life becomes uncentered.

The church must be active in helping believers establish meaningful goals and helping them be accountable for the fulfillment of these priorities. Eldon Trueblood, a great spiritual giant of the past century, began an organization called The Yokefellows where men held each other accountable for the spiritual disciplines in their lives: study, worship, prayer, time, money and spiritual gifts. We do well to help each other establish meaningful but flexible priorities and to be held accountable for their pursuit.

Setting free the practice of the gifts of the Spirit. Christ, the head of the church, gives gifts by the Holy Spirit to each believer for the work of ministry and the common good of the body of Christ. Among the lists of gifts (I Cor. 12, Rom. 12, Eph. 4) are the very practical service-oriented gifts such as hospitality, helping others, administration, giving, contributing to the needs of others and encouraging. This list certainly is not exhaustive. The church must always be finding practical ways to serve the King of the Kingdom faithfully. To be a teacher in the church, to be given the gift of a word of wisdom and knowledge, to have the gift of healing or deciphering tongues takes some maturity and seasoning. However, everyone must be active in doing good deeds. At one level, to do good deeds does not require a special calling; it simply needs to be done.

During the past decade a new touch of the Spirit has been evident in youth movements across the nation. Through "random acts of kindness", a slogan which plays off the dark North American news media sentence which laments the "random acts of violence" in society, the kindness and generosity of Christianity has once again begun to make an impact on our society. As good as this may be, the church needs more than random acts of kindness; it needs consistent acts of kindness. This consistency will only blossom and grow when the church intentionally brings faith and good deeds together. And God has equipped the church marvelously for such good works through the gifts of the Holy Spirit.

Illustrations of faith and good deeds are everywhere. James uses illustrations in a very consistent manner. He dips into the common history of the people of God to draw examples into the contemporary life of the church. Hebrews 11, for example, lists many such people out of the historical tradition of the Hebrew people. Each church tradition has its heroes of the faith, women and men who refused to give in to societal values and pressures to live faithful and exemplary lives. We do well to examine such lives and hold them up as role models for believers to follow.

The joy of a well-lived life. There is something infectious and freeing when we see Christians living life with vitality, enthusiasm and energy. The stereotyping of lifestyles has relegated the Christian lifestyle to the more boring, uninteresting side of things. The church needs to recapture the sheer energy and joy of living life well. It needs to develop a momentum around involvement in society, doing good wherever it is needed, touching those who are lonely and despairing with a word of encouragement. The demonstration of a buoyant, open-faced generosity toward life and those with whom we share our communities will become a powerful witness to the wholeness which has come into our lives.

Keeping belief sound, keeping good deeds relevant. The church has been very concerned about kerygmatic faithfulness; that is, it has been preoccupied with keeping heresy out of belief. This is a continuing need. Sound doctrine and a vital biblical faith are central to a faithful church. Because the battle for the evangelical faith is a never-ending battle, it seems as though the best energies of the church are directed to that conflict. Often conventions and conferences are called to determine what we believe about a spiritual matter, but rarely do we call conventions to develop a strategy for the spread of good deeds throughout the land. The church would be well served if we could gather together with the single agenda determining ways to make our good deeds as relevant as possible.

Personal Response

* The debate between Paul and James seems to not go away. Paul argues we are saved by faith without works; James argues good deeds validate our faith, and if there are no good deeds, then there obviously is no faith. DISCUSS: What do you think about all of this?

* The demons believe too, James argues, but their belief does not save them. DISCUSS: If a person were saved by belief/faith alone, does that mean demons might also be saved? Is James correct in alluding to this possibility?

* Abraham is cited as an example of having a saving-kind-of-

faith. God asked him to do an almost impossible thing, to sacrifice his son Isaac. He complied and intended to do it. DISCUSS: Check Hebrews 11:17-19 where we are given a glimpse into Abraham's thinking. What did Abraham put his faith in as he took Isaac on that fateful journey toward the mountain of sacrifice?

   * Rahab is a very interesting person who seems to have had a very prominent life within Israel after the fall of Jericho. Rahab lied to protect the spies hidden on the rooftop of her house. DISCUSS: Faith, good deeds and sometimes not telling the truth are part of the Rahab legacy. How do you sort out these things in your mind?

CHAPTER SEVEN

Controlling The Fire:
The Tongue

Not many of you should presume to be teachers, my brothers, because you know that we who teach will be judged more strictly. We all stumble in many ways. If anyone is never at fault in what he says, he is a perfect man, able to keep his whole body in check.

When we put bits into the mouths of horses to make them obey us, we can turn the whole animal. Or take ships as an example. Although they are so large and are driven by strong winds, they are steered by a very small rudder wherever the pilot wants to go. Likewise the tongue is a small part of the body, but it makes great boasts. Consider what a great forest is set on fire by a small spark. The tongue also is a fire, a world of evil among the parts of the body. It corrupts the whole person, sets the whole course of his life on fire, and is itself set on fire by hell.

All kinds of animals, birds, reptiles and creatures of the sea are being tamed and have been tamed by man, but no man can tame the tongue. It is a restless evil, full of deadly poison.

With the tongue we praise our Lord and Father, and with it we curse men, who have been made in God's likeness. Out of the same mouth come praise and cursing. My brothers, this should not be. Can both fresh water and salt water flow from the same spring? My brothers, can a fig tree bear olives, or a grapevine bear figs? Neither can a salt spring produce fresh water (James 3: 1-12).

The Flow and Form of the Text

One of the dominant characteristics of Hebraic preaching is its repetitive nature and the cyclical patterns of thought which the speaker returns to again and again. Each time a subject surfaces it is strengthened and additional material is brought to the topic. The twelve verses of this passage are a prime example of this intensification process. They pick up and strengthen the previous themes. In 1:19-21 the issue of anger expressed in words has been highlighted; in 1:26-28 the matter of empty, meaningless words is cited; and in 2:14-16 the abominable practice of using religious words to avoid putting Christian values into action is assailed.

Now James devotes almost all of these lines to a perspective on the nature of words and the tongue. The language of this text is so strong and the treatment of the subject matter so surprising that it almost takes one's breath away.

The flow of the text is not as logical or as easy to follow as the earlier texts. The course of the passage begins by moving toward one direction, but after the opening sentence quickly moves in another direction. This, of course, is the advantage of flow-of-consciousness preaching and writing in that it allows the writer to take the reader in the direction where the Spirit is leading.

The text opens safely enough with a caution directed toward teachers in the church. The intent of the caution is to express concern for careful, guarded speech but it is expressed in a most unusual manner. The caution takes the form of a negative prohibition and is cited in judgment terms: "Not many of you should presume to be teachers because you know that we who teach will be judged more strictly."

The text then moves through three phases: verses 3:3-6 are developed by two illustrations which make the case for the power of the tongue; verses 3:7-8 cite the wild and evil nature of the tongue; and verses 3:9-12 highlight the contrary, contradictory nature and behavior of the tongue. The style of the text is bombastic and grandiloquent. In order to make the point that the tongue is uncontrollable and entirely unruly, James engages in the same kind of bombastic, inflammatory, uncompromising language of which he himself accuses the tongue.

The Text Explained

The immediate impression created by this text is confusion. At the heart of James' rhetoric is the idea that the tongue is inherently evil and controls the person. Normally we would expect James to argue that the tongue is a reflection, a mirror of what a person truly is, what a person thinks and believes, and how a person behaves. Two statements moderate James' rhetoric on the nature of the tongue. The first concedes human fallibility: "We all stumble in many ways. If anyone is never at fault in what he says, he is a perfect man, able to keep his whole body in check" (3:2); and the second calls for a change in behavior: "My brothers, this should not be" (3:10b).

A stricter judgment (vv. 1-2) In typical flow-of-consciousness preaching, James opens this pericope with one idea but ends up preaching about something else. The opening sentence leads us to believe the subject matter will concern the nature of teaching and responsibilities associated with the role of teachers in the church. And indirectly this happens, but not intentionally. The caution which is issued takes on a negative form and is presented in terms of a stricter judgment on teachers than on other persons in the church.

The idea that a more severe judgment of God is tied to leadership roles in the church is alluded to in the New Testament in a vague, general way but is only explicitly stated in this text. Jesus concludes his warning on watchfulness with the words, "From everyone who has been given much, much will be demanded; and from the one who has been entrusted with much, much more will be asked" (Luke 12:47-48). This is the closest the New Testament comes to underscoring the point James is making here.

Two illustrations: the bridle and the rudder (vv. 3-6) The first illustration of the horse controlled by the bridle has roots in Old Testament literature (Ps. 32:8-10) where the metaphor is used to describe how the people of God ought not to behave. In our text, the metaphor is used to describe how a large animal can be controlled by something as small as a bridle. The second illustration, a small rudder controlling the direction of a great ship, reinforces this idea even more.

In both cases, the bridle and the rudder are seen in a positive light as both are under the control of humans and are useful to humanity. However, James uses these same metaphors to establish the point that the tongue, while having the power of a bridle and a rudder, controls and contaminates the body, and this in turn allows evil to run wild and unchecked.

No one will argue the power of the tongue, not only to set the direction for the human being but also to create chaos within human relationships. Therefore, when James exclaims "what a great forest is set on fire by a small spark" and likens the spark to the volatility of speech, few shake their heads in disagreement.

Where disagreement might come is in the next statement: "The tongue also is a fire, a world of evil among the parts of the body. It corrupts the whole person, sets the whole course of [their] life on fire, and is itself set on fire by hell."

The tongue has enormous power for actual harm. It might be a small body part but it certainly has the power to inflame passions, break relationships, mar friendships, and set the world aflame with hostility and anger. What is not at issue is whether it is the mind and thinking of believers which set the tongue on edge to do its dirty work; or whether it is the tongue, against the will of the believer, which sets in motion this beastly process of setting the forest on fire.

Alec Motyer, in a helpful comment on this text, notes four aspects of the fiery potency of the tongue. It starts with "character" in that the tongue "appoints itself as the world of unrighteousness among our members." It continues with "influence". Left to itself, because the tongue is so intensely involved in all the thoughts, longings and planning of life itself, it leaves the indelible stain of defilement on everything it touches. The third is "continuance". It has been noted that most vices are corrected by age or the passage of time. But the power and insidious maelstrom of the tongue continues unabated into old age. And fourth, it is "affiliated" with the fire of hell itself. The Valley of Henna was a garbage dump just outside the walls of Jerusalem. Night and day the fires burned, fed on the garbage of humanity. And so it is with the tongue. Ropes goes so far as to say that the very fires of hell itself ignite the paper-dry fuel of the tongue and everything explodes into flame.

The wild, untamable nature of the tongue (vv. 7-8) To the westernized reader of this text, the assertion that everything and anything can be tamed except the tongue seems to be stronger rhetoric than necessary. But as Adamson points out, Orientals give their tongues much more license than we do in our culture.

While it is true that every kind of beast, bird, reptile and creature has been successfully tamed, with many tamed to the point of being domesticated and useful to humanity, it also is true that the tongue cannot be tamed. The tongue, writes Michel, is a "monster of caprice". Sometimes at the slightest provocation, words are spoken which are hurtful and destructive, which the writer Jeremiah declares to be like "a bow and arrow that pierce the body" (9:3). Other times they are spoken with care but are full of deadly poison.

Mario Puzo in his novel *The Sicilian* (1985) has a telling line in which he describes the British in Sicily as those "who could be so subtly rude that you basked in their insults for days before you realized they had mortally wounded you". Indeed, the tongue is an unruly instrument of destruction and causes havoc whenever it is out of control.

The contradictory nature of the tongue (vv. 9-12) In this final section James creates five couplets of words, each describing an incompatible dualism. He makes the point that the tongue can produce both good and evil almost simultaneously from the same inner source. The tongue is driven by an inner spirit which makes the speaking believer rise to sublime heights and then plunged into the gorge of darkness. The five couplets - blessing and curse, praise and curse, salt water and fresh water, figs and olives, grapes and figs - reinforce the complexity and contrariness of the tongue and underscore its unmanageable nature

The Epistle of James has many connecting points to the Gospels, particularly the Gospel of Matthew. With the Sermon on the Mount, Jesus makes precisely the same point James is developing in this passage (Matt. 7:15-23). There is a difference, however. The context of Jesus' words is a warning against false teachers who come at the people of God in sheep's clothing but are ravenous wolves. In the Matthew text, the problem is not the tongue; rather, it is the inner life of the false teachers. Jesus makes the point that every person will eventually reveal what is truly within the inner spirit.

James, on the other hand, concedes that both evil and good come out of the same tongue. His stern comment, "My brothers [and sisters], this should not be" (3:10) concedes this is an unusual and not-to-be-expected behavior. However, as unacceptable as this may be, the reality is this is the way it often turns out.

One day Jesus confronted Peter, after the disciple offered what he thought to be good advice. Jesus' outburst, "Get behind me, Satan!" (Matt. 16:22-23), happened immediately after Peter had been complimented by Jesus for making the most sublime confession ever spoken by a human, a confession which Jesus declared to be from God himself: "You are the Christ, the Son of the living God!" (Matt. 16:16).

Application, Teaching/Preaching Points

This text is so full of rich material and so relevant to the life of the church that many application points can be made. Speech patterns and unruly words are probably behind more relationship trouble in society and the church than any other single factor. It is appropriate that sermons, Bible study lessons and Sunday School curriculum be fashioned around this topic. Here are five simple truths which will bring these living words from the pages of the Scriptures into the lives of the people of God.

The responsible role of being a teacher in the church. One of the gifts of leadership in the church is the role of teacher (Eph. 4:11-13). Without gifted teachers who open the Scriptures and nurture the inner spirit of followers of Jesus, the church remains without direction and becomes less than it should be. James wants every teacher to approach the task of teaching with great caution and serious intent. Not all roles in the church are equal. To be a teacher means one must accept responsibility not only for the material which is taught, but also for the life which is lived.

If one major truth surfaces again and again in this epistle it is that belief and lifestyle and belief, vocation and ethics must be in harmony. The reason why teachers will be judged by a more strict standard is because teaching and personal lifestyle are inseparably tied together. To teach and not to live what is being taught is to undo that which is being taught.

The New Testament church was always on guard against false teachers. There were those who tried to reintroduce Judaism back into the Christian message (Gal. 1:6-17); there were the novices who wanted to teach but did not yet possess the maturity and understanding to be effective (I Tim. 1:6ff), and there were those whose lives simply did not measure up and who threatened to bring dishonor on the church (Rom. 2:17-29). The church must always be on guard against false teachers who threaten to lead the people of God astray. It must also warn its teachers about the standard which God requires of them because they will be measured by a stricter judgment.

The fallibility of humanity. James opens the epistle by asserting that life is a series of trials (1:2ff) and to cope successfully with these trials each believer needs the wisdom of God. In a backhanded sort-of-way, James implies that humanity is not infallible, there are many traps and sideshows which detract the believer from living life as richly as it ought to be lived.

In this passage, James strengthens the idea that we all need wisdom because of our sinfulness. Our lack of perfection is symbolized by our inability to keep our "whole body in check".

There is nothing particularly new in all of this. Very few persons go through life thinking themselves to be infallible. Every person who becomes a part of the community of faith understands very quickly that "we all stumble in many ways". This is not to say that all sin is intentional. Sin and sinning are often more a floundering around than a planned thing. Such sinfulness is part of the dynamic which shapes the ethos of the body of Christ. We do well to acknowledge our failures and sins and confess that we are sinners. But it is usually unwise to interpret every sin which occurs in the flow of everyday life to be more than it truly is. Paul speaks about "bear[ing] with each other" (Col. 3:13). In other words, he notes, put up with some things in the church and in personal relationships! This is not to say that we ought to be soft on sin. The point is that if we acknowledge our sinfulness and recognize that many of our sins are simply "the sins of the way" (Stulac), it will make us easier to live with in the fellowship of believers. Forgiveness is the grace to accept the weakness and frailty of human conduct and experience.

An out-of-control tongue is a beastly thing. When speech is seasoned and controlled it is a blessing and a force for good. When the tongue is controlled, speech is hardly noticed. However, when speech is abrasive, cutting and caustic it is very much noticed and becomes a divisive curse in society and the church. Little wonder Jesus proclaimed, "By your words you shall be justified and by your words you shall be condemned" (Matt. 12:36-37) and the Old Testament sage noted, "A gentle answer turns away wrath, but a harsh word stirs up anger" (Prov. 15:1) and "The words that bring healing are a tree of life, but a deceitful tongue crushes the spirit" (Prov. 15:4).

James is not saying silence is better than speech, although he earlier cautioned against too many words. He is not making a case for silence, but since words have such immense power, the Christian ought to be very careful how they are used. The Jewish rabbis in Jesus' day had a wonderful saying: "Life and death are in the hand of the tongue. Has the tongue a hand? No, but as the hand kills, so does the tongue!"

Blessing and cursing. In her novel *The Scots* (1984) Jane Toombs describes a man who represents all that is good and evil, noble and ignoble, heroic and cowardly, divine and earthly in humanity.

James concurs. Out of the same mouth, he writes, comes cursing and blessing. What James has in mind is the mindset that allows a Christian to praise God joyfully at one time and to be harsh, unforgiving and rude at other times. While each person has been given the full range of emotions from the truest love which leads a person to die for another to the foulest anger which causes violence and murder, it is also true that having the capacity for such radically different emotions and behaviors does not give the believer permission to move easily from one extreme to the other.

Paul emphasizes that the fruit of the Spirit includes self-control (Gal. 5:22). Self-control ought not to be a denial of the vitality and passion for life which is born into every human being, but it ought to help focus life so we do not live at the whim of passions which allow us to soar to the greatest heights and the next moment plunge into the darkest abyss.

The mouth speaks what is in the heart. Each person is a complex mix of personality and spirituality. Each person in the fellowship of the church responds to the events of life in differing ways. Some persons are of quiet, soft-spoken disposition and more careful with words, rarely being volatile in speech or behavior. Others are more expressive. Their words tumble out in torrents. The Scriptures are full of warnings about the conflict that rages within each person regardless of personality. Paul informs the church that the Spirit of God and the spirit of our humanness, called the works of the flesh, are in conflict with each other (Gal. 5:16-25). Jesus taught his disciples it is not what goes into the mouth which contaminates them but what comes out of the heart (Matt. 15:10); it is out of the abundance of the heart that a person speaks (Matt. 12:34).

Ultimately, what matters most is the condition of the heart; that is, the degree of Spirit-control and spiritual maturity which has come to the believer. The greater the maturity of the believer the less likely it will be that speech, the true mirror of a person's inner life, will be unsavory and damaging to relationships.

Personal Response

* This passage opens with a most amazing sentence. James seems to argue that not many people should become teachers in the church because of the stricter judgment which will applied to them. DISCUSS: Is this a good enough reason to keep someone from aspiring to become a teacher in the church?

* James notes that "we all stumble in many ways" (3:2a). Another way of saying the same thing is that sinfulness is part of our existence. Salvation grants us the gift of salvation, and the process of spiritual maturity is simply becoming what we have already been declared to be in Christ. It is usually agreed there are three

kinds of sins in our lives: the inadvertent sins of simply living, the besetting sins which cling to us and are hard to shake, and the intentional sins of the high hand. DISCUSS: What is the difference between these kinds of sins? Should the church respond differently to each kind of sin, or is sin always sin? How do you think God looks on these differing kinds of sin?

* The tongue is said to be "a world of evil among the parts of the body ... set on fire by hell". DISCUSS: Is the problem the tongue, or are we the problem?

* Strange as it might be, we bless God and then defame God with our speech. The fact that we are not perfect can be a dreadnought on our soul keeping us from praising God our Savior. DISCUSS: It has been noted that the church is comprised of hypocrites who proclaim a good news gospel more energetically than they live the gospel in life. Do you agree? Should our sinfulness keep us from worshipping God?

CHAPTER EIGHT

Only One Of Two Ways:
Earthly Or Heavenly Wisdom

Who is wise and understanding among you? Let him show it by his good life, by deeds done in the humility that comes from wisdom. But if you harbor bitter envy and selfish ambition in your hearts, do not boast about it or deny the truth. Such "wisdom" does not come down from heaven but is earthly, unspiritual, of the devil. For where you have envy and selfish ambition, there you find disorder and every evil practice.

But the wisdom that comes from heaven is first of all pure; then peace loving, considerate, submissive, full of mercy and good fruit, impartial and sincere. Peacemakers who sow in peace raise a harvest of righteousness (James 3:13-18).

The Flow and Form of the Text

This text is connected to the previous material both in form and content. The earlier text concluded with a series of rhetorical questions which demanded a negative answer: "Can both fresh water and salt water flow from the same well?" and "Can a fig tree bear olives, or a grapevine bear figs?"

The opening question of this text follows hard on these two rhetorical questions. The question here is not answered by a simple "yes" or "no". It requires more reflection because it is a question of motivation and inner well-being. James' answer is an enrichment and deepening of two themes encountered earlier: wisdom and good works. In 1:2-8 the theme of wisdom is developed in considerable detail. True wisdom comes from God and is available to every believer simply by asking (1:5). However, godly wisdom is not the only kind of wisdom available to the believing person. In this passage wisdom is seen to come from two sources. Some wisdom is earthly, unspiritual and comes from the devil himself. Such wisdom is to be avoided. Contrasted to this earthly wisdom is the wisdom which comes from heaven which, by implication, is from God.

The specific deeds that are produced within us by following earthly wisdom are not detailed for the reader as they are in some other New Testament writings (Gal. 5:19-21; I Peter 2:1). Rather, James gets at the root cause for all the unsettledness which such wisdom creates. He argues that bitter envy and selfish ambition are at the center of earthly wisdom. Whenever these two vices, which L.E. Maxwell once called "the devil's glittering twins," are practiced, there you will find the fruit of earthly wisdom - disorder and all kinds of evil practice. Heavenly wisdom is then contrasted to earthly wisdom. Eight characteristics are cited.

The passage ends with the resounding affirmation that heavenly wisdom will always produce an abundant "harvest of righteousness", which is to be contrasted to the chaos and every kind of evil which earthly wisdom produces.

The Text Explained

It is important to review what James means when he writes about wisdom. The word "wisdom" in the English language has adopted a wide range of meanings. Many of these meanings we also find in the Scriptures. In the Old Testament wisdom can mean everything from the ability to do skillful, artistic work (Ex. 28:3; 31:3), to having understanding, insight and prudence (Prov. 3:2; I Chron. 22:12), to the sagacious behavior which enables a person to master life's complexities (Prov. 8:32-36). All of these meanings are incorporated into current modern thought and language.

But there is one meaning of wisdom which is only found in biblical thinking and, although it is common in the Scriptures, it is only understood by those who know God and follow him. In our world the opposite of being wise is to be unwise or foolish, which has more to do with the choices we make than the persons we are.

In the Old Testament the opposite of being wise is to be a fool, and a fool is a person who willingly and intentionally pushes God out of the center of life. Therefore, the writers of the Proverbs, Psalms and Job can repeatedly argue that the beginning of wisdom lies in knowledge of God (Prov. 1:7; 9:10; Job 28:28; Ps. 111:10), and the Psalmist can cry out in alarm, "The fool has said in his heart, 'There is no God!'" (Ps. 14:1; 53:1).

The prohibition by Jesus against calling one's brother a fool (Matt. 5:22) means we cannot flay foolish deeds; rather, if a fool is a person who has removed God from the center of life, we then by calling a person a fool infringe on God's right — a right which the Eternal Lord refuses to share with anyone — to judge who is and who is not a godly person. Ultimately only God knows such things.

Wisdom and a good life (v. 13) "Who among you is wise?" is the question which opens this passage. The answer is surprisingly easy to understand: "The ones who by their good lives and good deeds do what wisdom demands!" In other words, having God centered in our lives ought to make a big difference in how we live. James makes the point it is good people who are wise — the people who have God in their lives and who live and serve with great humility.

Conversely the unwise are the ones who do not live good lives nor do they produce good deeds in humility. This text confronts us with a choice. James follows the teaching of Jesus by asserting there are only two ways to live. Jesus set the terms of reference in this matter. He taught there are only two roads, one broad and easy, the other narrow and difficult (Matt. 7:13-14). Jesus proclaimed it will be either God or mammon which will control our affections (Matt. 6:24); our lives will be characterized by two choices, good or bad fruit (Matt. 7:15-20); we build our lives either in the wadi where destruction will suddenly overwhelm us, or we will build on the rock where security will be our lot (Matt. 7:24-27). In this text, like in Jesus' own words, there are two ways of living with no middle ground to blend them together.

Earthly wisdom, or the wisdom which is from the devil (vv. 14-16) At the heart of earthly wisdom is the self-centeredness of humanity. Two colorful descriptive terms are introduced to the reader which describe the wisdom that is from the devil. In both cases, the wisdom of the devil is seen to improve the lot of the person who practices it but in the end reaps what it has sown - chaos and destruction.

The first of these two couplets is "bitter envy", bitter being the adjective which describes or modifies the noun envy. The Greek word *zelos* can be translated either as envy or jealous. *Zelos* was understood originally to be a neutral word; that is, it can be either positive or negative. Envy in the positive sense can drive a person to aspire to greater deeds and effort. In the negative sense, it can describe an attitude of begrudging what another person possesses or has attained.

It is well to be reminded that there is a very fine line between noble aspiration and ignoble envy or jealousy. Usually it is the context or the adjective which precedes it which determines its meaning. In the case of this combination, the context of envy makes it negative, and adding the adjective bitter makes it thoroughly negative.

The word bitter has a long colorful history. At first it simply meant distasteful and was used to describe fruits, vegetables and spices which were tart and unpleasant to the taste. It was also used to describe the stagnant water which gathered in low places in the desert. During the rainy season these low places would fill with water and as summer came, they would slowly become foul, stinking water holes.

Soon a metaphorical meaning began to emerge. The word was used to describe the tragic and painful experiences of life. Some translations use bitter to describe the pain and grief which Esau and his two wives, Judith and Basemath, brought to Isaac and Rebekah (Gen. 26:35).

So when James uses the word bitter as an adjective it has a metaphorical meaning. It describes an attitude as foul as the brackish, polluted waters of the desert, a rottenness which has settled into the core of human existence.

The second combination, selfish ambition, is like the first. The noun ambition is a neutral word describing the drive to succeed which is born in each of us. Ambition *eritheia* has a very interesting history. At first it simply meant spinning for hire, then it came to mean the work which is done for pay. From here it began to describe an attitude which sees work only in terms of what a person can get out of it. And finally, it entered political life where it described the intrigue and intent to use any means to arrive at an end. By the time James uses this word, it has a decidedly negative ring. Our English word selfish reinforces this idea and suggests that the sole object of ambition is to enhance one's own position.

If the biblical definition of wisdom is the art of keeping God in the center of life, then selfish ambition is the sin of placing one's own values and importance ahead of God. Such behavior the Psalmist would surely declare to be foolishness.

The source and final end of such wisdom concludes this paragraph. James wants his readers to be very clear about the origin of all self-centered behavior and religion. Such wisdom is from below, not above; therefore it is "earthly, unspiritual, of the devil". The legacy of such earthly wisdom is found in the competitive, disorderly world where everything revolves around the self-centered practice of looking out only for oneself.

The devil is named only twice in the entire epistle, here and in 4:7. In this passage the devil is seen as the one who creates an illusion of upward mobility and the importance of self-serving enterprise. As with all sinful behavior, the devil encourages the taking of good, creative human energies and refocusing them toward selfish ends. In 4:7 the devil is personalized as the opponent of God. But fleeing into the refuge of God distances the Christian from the influence and power of the devil; conversely, to draw near to the devil is to be separated from God.

Heavenly wisdom, or the wisdom which comes from God (vv. 17-18) James uses eight words to describe heavenly wisdom. The list is a veritable "who's who" of virtue. These eight words — pure, peace loving, considerate, submissive, merciful, good fruit, impartial and sincere — are the legendary stuff of a rich, good, godly life. Pure describes transparent, authentic, unmixed, unalloyed goodness; peace loving means not only the absence of conflict but also the ability to help another attain all of the goodness which God has intended for humanity; considerate is the ability to see the good in deeds and in persons, and to treat every human being with dignity; submissive reflects the grace of not lording it over those whom we can naturally intimidate, or the ability to accept correction (Manton) or another's idea; merciful is forgiving freely and letting go of that which holds people in bondage; good fruit stands in opposition to the works of the flesh; impartial is the willingness to discern fairly in complex matters and to treat each person with the same respect; and sincere reflects an attitude of humility.

This is what James has been working toward from the opening sentence of this epistle and what he wants for the people of God scattered throughout the world. This is the heart of his cry for justice, strong faith and good deeds. These eight virtues describe all the qualities of a controlled tongue, a life rich in faith and deeds, a just life where rich and poor alike can live in respect and harmony, and a life which has God in the center of everything.

The concluding sentence of this section, "Peacemakers who sow in peace raise a harvest of righteousness," informs the readers that planting time always comes before harvest and whatever we sow, we also will reap. The idea of sowing and reaping is a well-worn biblical metaphor. Most of the sayings in the Book of Proverbs work on this principle. Jesus added his weight to this metaphor by telling the parable of a sower and the seed (Luke 8:4-8, 11-15), and Paul reminds readers that sowing and reaping are inseparably tied together (Gal. 6:7-8).

James concludes this passage by putting the emphasis on being peacemakers. Earlier he has listed "peace loving" as the fruit of heavenly wisdom, which is a condition of the heart and an attitude of the mind. This is important because James has argued earlier that what is in the heart of a person will determine action. Peacemaking is putting "peace loving" into action. Again, James is very concerned that belief finds its way into lifestyle. For this church statesman, to be peace loving means to be a peacemaker.

Peace and well-being are set up as an alternative to the combativeness and chaos created by earthly wisdom. Peacemaking is contrasted to bitter envy and selfish ambition, the deceptive lollipops marketed by the devil. The struggle for supremacy between earthly and heavenly wisdom is a constant battle. It is fought in the mind and will of every Christian believer.

Application, Teaching/Preaching Points

This passage is full of practical spiritual advice on how to live the abundant life. James names the problem with clarity and provides solutions which will help the believer to live a good life. Four points merit some comment.

A caution against harboring bitter envy and selfish ambition. The Greek reading of "but if you have bitter jealousy in your heart" gets right to the heart of the matter. Bitter jealousy is something that lies deep within the human spirit. If it is there, it will not lie dormant forever; it will eventually burst out into the open. Bitterness, foulness of spirit and jealousy are symptoms. The problem is the heart. Actions are merely the outward demonstration of the values which govern our thinking. The answer to changed behavior lies in changing the source of our wisdom.

The answer to bitter envy and selfish ambition is not to call on people to clean up their act. It is to find a new source of wisdom, a source which will renew the inner spirit so what lies deeply within the human heart will find positive expression in life.

The nature of spiritual warfare. From the earliest days of humanity the conflict between good and evil, God and the devil, has raged relentlessly. This war has been called "the conflict of the ages" and has been with us for a long, long time. In recent years much attention has been focused on this conflict. "Spiritual warfare" has become one of the new buzzwords in the evangelical church, and thus a greater emphasis of the nature of the conflict between God and the devil has been created. The individual believer and the church must be constantly alert to the danger of falling into the snare of the Evil One. However, more importantly, the individual believer and the church must be reminded of the power of God to help everyone live a victorious life.

Most of this emphasis on spiritual warfare is good, but there is also danger in overemphasizing it. Too often spiritual warfare language has been used to avoid taking responsibility for one's actions. Sometimes the sense is the devil makes us do things we do not want to do and we are helplessly under the influence and control of the Evil One. James reminded us how insidious and how quickly sin grows and develops within the believer (1:13-16).

This passage sets out the nature of earthly wisdom and heavenly wisdom, and names the source of each. And we must decide and choose which wisdom we are to follow. Choosing is not something that can be done for us. We can avoid making the choice, but in not choosing, we choose anyway.

Choices are usually most easily made when the options are clearly articulated for us. Gifted teachers in the church are responsible for the task of setting out the implications of the choices we make. The reading, studying and meditating on the Scriptures is a lifeline which rescues us from popular myths. The slogan "the devil made me do it" is a myth that only has credence when there is an absence of teaching in the church.

The leadership of the church must exercise great care so the truth of the Scriptures is constantly placed before the members of the body of Christ, making sure the options available are highlighted and good choices can be encouraged.

A call to goodness. There is an innate tug towards selfishness, self-centeredness and self-preservation which gets in the way of good, godly living. Goodness never comes easily or naturally to us. To do good and live a life rich in faith requires a constant facing up to pressure because our natural inclinations are to go with the flow. Burton Hillis once noted, "Experience teaches that love of flowers and vegetables is not enough to make people become good gardeners. They must also hate weeds!"

This text calls every believer to a life guided by heavenly wisdom, where virtues like purity, peace, mercy, sincerity and impartiality are practiced as a normal part of life. This always requires intentional choice and deliberate action. Every good deed stands in opposition to some self-serving or base deed. Purity, for example, is the opposite of impurity. Purity is hard to maintain because the world in which we live contaminates everything it touches. The opposite of sincerity is phoniness. Sincerity is hard to maintain as believers are bombarded with requests for compassion and few are truly interested in becoming involved with others. Jesus, with his parable on the Good Samaritan, pointed out it is always easier to walk away from something than to take a sincere interest in it.

Sowing and reaping. The Scriptures are full of sowing and reaping language; that is, every action has a consequence. Paul warns we ought not to be deceived into thinking God can be mocked or fooled, because what we have sown earlier, we reap (Gal. 6:7-8).

The pattern of sowing and reaping is both a biblical principle as well as a commonsense law. James says if a person wants to create a harvest of righteousness, it must be sown in peace. This fact, however, ought not to lull us into a position where all the events of life and history are interpreted as reaping what has been sown. The patriarch Job was immersed in trouble and grief by events not of his own making. He was not aware of the conversation between God and Satan concerning his blameless life. If he had known it might have made his suffering more tolerable. However, he constantly and consistently refused to accept the arguments of his friends that his troubles were due to his sin. In some cases, what we reap is not of our making.

Jesus was asked by his disciples whether the blind man they had just encountered was in this condition through his own sin or the sins of his parents (John 9:1-41). Jesus gives an amazing answer: "Neither." Great care must be given in the church not to connect each event of life to an action. Some very good things which are not of our making come into our lives anyway. They are undeserved and are a gift from God to us. Conversely, some dreadful things come to us which also are not of our making nor deserved.

Many of the circumstances of our lives come to us simply because we participate in the happiness and sorrow of a fallen world. Disease, debilitating old age, accidents, natural disasters and the disasters created by humanity's inhumanity to people are part of living in our world. Sometimes these traumatic events flood into our lives and we are immersed in pain and discomfort. At times like this the comfort of a caring God is needed to help heal the hurt inflicted by daily living.

However, having noted the truth of all these things, we ought not to minimize the principle of sowing and reaping. Each action has consequences.

Personal Response

   * James, like Jesus, announces there are only two options for our lives: follow either earthly wisdom or heavenly wisdom. DISCUSS: In our modern way of thinking we like to have more than only two options. Is this analysis too narrow for us? Is there a third way? Is there a bridge between the two options?

   * Ambition is not a bad word in our society. It describes the drive to create, achieve and conquer obstacles. Most great advances in technology and medical science have come because skilled people have refused to give in to failure. In our text, the word "ambition" only occurs in the section describing earthly wisdom. DISCUSS: We are aware that when "selfish" is added to "ambition", only bad things are likely to happen. However, can ambition ever be laundered so it becomes a virtue in our lives?

   * James lists eight virtues which are produced by following and practicing heavenly wisdom. Look at the list: pure, peace loving, considerate, submissive, full of mercy, full of good fruit, impartial and sincere. DISCUSS: Cite some practical ways in which these can be brought to maturity in our lives and in the collective life of the church.

   * Sowing and reaping is a biblical principle which we ought not ignore. Most of the time it is in force. Other times it is not. DISCUSS: Is it ever right to announce to someone "I told you so" when reaping begins to happen? How is this different from judging people?

   * Job's friends were adamant that Job's trials were the result of his sinfulness. They were wrong. Job, who steadfastly declared his innocence, ended up being right. God vindicated him. DISCUSS: How do we work with people who, for no apparent reason, appear to have one bad thing after another happen to them?

CHAPTER NINE

Bringing Out The Worst In Us:
On Fights, Feuds And Quarrels

What causes fights and quarrels among you? Don't they come from your desires that battle within you? You want something but don't get it. You kill and covet, but you cannot have what you want. You quarrel and fight. You do not have, because you do not ask God. When you ask, you do not receive, because you ask with wrong motives, that you may spend what you get on your pleasures.

You adulterous people, don't you know that friendship with the world is hatred toward God? Anyone who chooses to be a friend of the world becomes an enemy of God. Or do you think Scripture says without reason that the spirit he caused to live in us tends toward envy, but he gives us more grace? That is why Scripture says: "God opposes the proud but gives grace to the humble."

Submit yourselves, then, to God. Resist the devil, and he will flee from you. Come near to God and he will come near to you. Wash your hands, you sinners, and purify your hearts, you double-minded. Grieve, mourn and wail. Change your laughter to mourning and your joy to gloom. Humble yourselves before the Lord, and he will lift you up.

Brothers, do not slander one another. Anyone who speaks against his brother or judges him, speaks against the law and judges it. When you judge the law, you are not keeping it, but sitting in judgment on it. There is only one Lawgiver and Judge, the one who is able to save and destroy. But you — who are you to judge your neighbor? (James 4:1-12)

The Flow and Form of the Text

The twelve verses which comprise this discreet unit can almost be called an omnibus text; that is, it is full of related commands and prohibitions which, if we would deal with them separately, would create a very difficult patchwork of teaching. Taken together, it makes more sense.

James intensifies the rhetoric which has already taken on a more intense, strident tone, beginning with a pungent discourse on the nature of speech and the power of the tongue. Beginning with 3:1 and carrying on to 5:6, the writing almost shouts at the reader. The language is loud and confronting; it is bombastic and full of warning; it is intense and unrelenting.

This passage separates into four terse paragraphs, each standing alone but also related to each other. The opening lines are very closely related to the earlier section and have long lines leading the reader back to the opening verses of the epistle.

The text begins with two questions which follow hard on James' assertion that all "disorder and evil practice" is the result of practicing earthly wisdom (3:14-16). The quarreling and fighting is driven by selfish ambition, to which he has already referred (3:13-16). Earthly wisdom and selfish ambition are interpreted as pursuing that which "you cannot have" but "you want". The phrase "you do not ask God" takes us back to 1:5 where believers are encouraged to "ask God" who will give wisdom generously to all those who ask. The phrase "you ask with wrong motives" harkens to 1:7 where the "double-minded, unstable" person is not granted an answer to prayer.

The second paragraph begins with a thunderous "You adulterous people," reminding the readers of the bold, provocative judgment speeches of the eighth century prophets who accused the people of God of spiritual harlotry. In this text the problem is not strange gods but friendship with the world. The question cited in 4:5 is notoriously difficult to interpret because the point which James attributes to the Scriptures is nowhere to be found in the Bible. Furthermore, the latter part of verse 5 is also very difficult to translate. Most marginal readings will add two other options for this verse, and no consensus exists in the way our English

Bibles translate this.   James concludes with a quotation of Proverbs 3:34 which opens the next topic in this omnibus text.

The third paragraph is a pastoral exhortation to "put-off" and "put-on". The "put-off" part is described by a plethora of action verbs like resist, wash, purify, grieve, mourn, wail and change. The "put-on" part is characterized by words like submit, come near and humble yourselves. The use of ten imperatives emphasizes that these are not to be viewed as suggestions; they are commands which ought to be obeyed.

The fourth paragraph reintroduces the matter of the tongue for the fifth time in this short epistle. This time the issue is slander and the law. In a clever way, James ties together Jesus' prohibition against judging others (Luke 6:37-42) with his own understanding of the denigration of the law. However, it is not so much the law which is central to this text, it is the Lawgiver, the Judge. God is central to this text, reinforcing once again the theocentric rather than Christocentric nature of this epistle.

The Text Explained

On fights, quarrels and selfishness (vv. 1-3) At the heart of all conflict, James concludes, is the civil war which rages within every believer. James uses two words to describe the nature of this civil war: there are wars which describe the global, unending conflict within us; and there are fights which describe the individualized skirmishes of the war. In other words, the war is unending and is played out in localized skirmishes, in which everything from pettiness and smallness to the more substantive, ideological conflicts are involved.

The lines of battle involve that which "you want" but "cannot have", and contentment. The contentment part is unspoken in this text but exists in the mind of James. Contentment and selfishness are not easy bedfellows. Paul the Apostle sets out the terms of this internal civil war in more informative language. He speaks about living "by the Spirit" as the positive part and gratifying "the desires of the sinful nature", the negative part (Gal. 5:16-18).

Earlier James has informed the readers that "fresh water and salt water" cannot flow from the same spring (3:11). In this passage, the problem is "asking with wrong motives" in order to "spend what you get on your pleasures." The asking and the intention to live in a self-indulgent manner indicates what is within the inner spirit of the person. The greed which marks the situation James alludes to is so strong that persons are prepared to "kill and covet" to get what they want. This strengthens the earlier notion that what is sown in the lives of believers will inevitably and invariably find its way into life and lifestyle.

God is good and generous (1:2-8) but God is not gullible, nor will he accommodate our insatiable desire for more possessions and things. The prayers which God answers positively are those which make us wiser and perfect, lacking in nothing and not adding to the wealth which allows the believer to live an overindulgent life.

The world: friend or foe? (vv. 4-6) James uses the vocative case with "My brothers" or "My dear brothers", or simply "brothers" 12 times. This is to be understood as addressing the church, both male and female. Five times, however, he uses the vocative case to address a very specific group of people. Each time he uses a different phrase. In the first occurrence, James opens with "You foolish man" (2:20); next he shouts "you adulterous people" (4:4); in 4:8 he ties together "you sinners" and "you double-minded"; and finally he will shout "You rich people" (5:1). Each of these five phrases has a distinct meaning and nuance. To be foolish is to be badly mistaken about something, either intentionally or inadvertently; to be adulterous is to be joined in an illicit relationship, thereby undermining the integrity of an earlier commitment; to be a sinner means that the former state from which the readers have been redeemed is still in force; to be double-minded means to be uncentered in life; and to be rich defines a particular class of society.

James opens this paragraph with the most powerful, extreme indictment available to him. "You adulterous people" is the thundering charge of unfaithfulness which the Old Testament prophets hurled at Israel (Hosea). It was this whoring after other lovers, other gods, which eventually resulted in the destruction of the nation and the temple.

At issue in this text is not the whoring after other gods; rather, it is cozying up to the world so friendship is possible. The logic James uses is simple, classic logic. If friendship with the world is hatred toward God, then it follows that to be a friend of the world is to be an enemy of God.   Like in the words of Jesus himself, James follows the New Testament argument that there are only two ways, the broad and the narrow; two places to build, on sand or on rock; and two options for a center in life, mammon (money) or God.

For the most part, the writing of James, while not easy to put into practice, is quite easy to understand. There is nothing particularly complex and mystifying about this epistle. However, there is one exception — it is 4:5. It is difficult on two counts: first, the sentence when translated is difficult to understand because it is not a complete sentence; and second, James prefaces this verse with the comment: "the Scripture says" which leads the reader to believe he is either quoting or paraphrasing an Old Testament text.

Concerning the first problem verse 5 is almost non-translatable as a sentence. This is how it appears translated literally word by word from the Greek text: **"with jealousy desiring the spirit which he caused to dwell in us."**

It is not a complete sentence and something appears to be lacking. Here is a sampling of the variety of ways in which the English Bible translates this impossible sentence. The New International *1976* Version says "the spirit he caused to live in us tends toward envy." You will notice that spirit is lower case, meaning it is the human spirit, not the Holy Spirit, which tends toward envy. The translators of the NIV make spirit the subject of the sentence. *1985. the changed*

The New Revised Standard Version translates it , "God yearns jealously for the spirit he has made to dwell in us." God is made to be the subject of the sentence, and the intent of the translation leans in the direction to present God as the One who yearns for fellowship with the human spirit.

The New American Standard Bible turns this phrase into a question: "He jealously desires the Spirit which He made to dwell in us?" The pronoun "he" becomes the subject of the sentence and

"Spirit" is capitalized, referring to the Holy Spirit, not the human spirit. These translators understand this sentence to mean that God is keenly interested in the work of the Holy Spirit in the believer — the Spirit which he placed in the Christian.

The Good News Bible changes the meaning again. "The spirit that God placed in us is filled with fierce desires" seems to indicate that the spirit (lower case) that God placed into humanity is full of intense desires.

And the Revised New English Bible tries to clarify this sentence with "the spirit which God implanted with us is filled with envious longings", which follows the Good News Bible but is less dramatic in its reading.

Concerning the second problem, we are confounded by James' assertion, "Or do you think the Scripture says without reason ..." when there is no apparent or obvious Scriptural text which says what 4:5b seems to say. If this were a quotation from some Old Testament text, we might be able to reconstruct with more accuracy the meaning of this.

What does all of this mean? The bottom line seems to be that God wants to work with humanity so believers will be transformed by God's all-encompassing grace. The clinching sentence, "but he (God) gives more grace" is the wonderful promise that God can and does supersede all of our "envious longings" (RNEB), every "tendency toward envy" (NIV), and every yearning of God through "the spirit he made to dwell in us" (NRSV). God does give grace to the humble, but the proud, the arrogant, the self-centered, the self-sufficient God will oppose.

Putting off and putting on (vv. 7-10) These three verses contain more commands and imperatives than any other similar section of writing in James. Ten times James issues a command. The commands fall into two general categories, although they are so complementary and integrated it is hard to make the case that they are only putting off or putting on. This text revolves around the things which should be done to get rid of unwise, corrupt living, and things which should be done to increase godliness. The action of putting off a vice must be followed by the action of putting on a virtue.

The opening sentence, "Submit yourselves to God" sets the agenda. The concluding command, "Humble yourselves before the Lord and he will lift you up" is the promise that God will not leave the believer in an unchanged state.

The other eight commands (resist the devil, come near to God, wash your hands, purify your hearts, grieve, mourn, wail and change your laughter into mourning) are a colorful kaleidoscope of images to make the point that unless some very intentional actions are taken to get sinful behavior and the influence of the devil out of the believer's life, things will mainly stay as they are. Fights and quarrels will continue, selfishness, coveting and greed will run amok, and friendship with the world will be seen as normative in the community of faith.

On slander, judging one another, and the Lawgiver (vv. 11-12)
The sequence of five steps in this paragraph are quite easy to follow except for one sentence. The paragraph opens with a prohibition against slander which is easy enough to understand.

The next step is the problem. James' argues that by speaking against a brother, the brother is judged and this in turn speaks against or judges the law. That the law is broken by the intentional slander of the brother is obvious. Just how the law is judged by slander is hard to understand. Some careful readers think James might be recalling the ninth commandment: "You shall not give false testimony against your neighbor" (Ex. 20:16). If the law is deliberately and intentionally broken, then the people breaking the law have set themselves over the law and in that they have judged it. This might be a somewhat circuitous way of explaining this sentence, but for many it seems to work reasonably well.

The final three steps of the progression are logical and easy to understand. When the law is judged by the believer not keeping it, the lawbreakers have set themselves over it; there is only one Lawgiver and Judge; and in the words of James himself: "But you — who are you to judge your neighbor?"

Application, Teaching/Preaching Points
In the opening paragraphs of this chapter, it was noted that sometimes   flow-of-consciousness   preaching   leads   the

writer/preacher in a direction which creates an almost contradictory conclusion to what the opening sentence promised. In this passage James has been very bold and harsh condemning the fights, feuds and quarrels which are part of the community of faith. He is, of course, justified in his criticisms. He has hurled a strong epitaph at the dispersed people, calling them, "You adulterous people." The language he has used is bombastic and very strong.

It is good for all readers and teachers in the church who wish to be faithful to the text, to acknowledge there is a fine line between judging the neighbor and the prophetic mission in preaching, where vivid descriptions of the sins of a people are verbalized so a call to repentance can be issued. While church leaders and teachers ought not to be discouraged from taking on the gods which beset this age, great care ought to be exercised so that the warning spoken to teachers in the church by James is a guiding principle in all teaching and nurturing activities of the community of faith.

Five strong teaching/preaching points emerge from this omnibus text. All are critical to the life of a healthy congregation. All are necessary for wholesome relationships to blossom within the fellowship of believers and in relationship to God.

Taking on the gods of greed and dissension. We live in a self-indulgent society where the quest for more and more is driven relentlessly by a consumer society. Advertising is designed to create need. What a person needs for a satisfying life is increasingly determined by dissatisfaction of what a person presently possesses. Enough somehow is never enough. Great care must be given to balance ambition with the values of wholeness and contentment. Contentment can lull a people to sleep; ambition can easily destroy contentment.

John Dean, in *Blind Ambition* (1976), a personal biography of sacrifice and achievement during the Watergate era in American political life, tells what happens when everything becomes negotiable and almost everything is sacrificed to gain a certain goal in life. Ethics always take a beating when the pursuit of a goal is stronger than the restraints which govern honor and the dignity of life itself.

Quarreling, fighting and feuding are born and sustained in the family and the church when achieving goals and accumulating assets become the prime virtues in life.

Prayers and the pleasures of self-indulgence. Riches are a gift from God. Sin in the Bible is always taking the good gifts of God and driving them to excess. William Barclay wisely makes the point that sin is simple taking the good things of life and making them into gods. Adultery is using God's gift of sex in illicit relationships; gluttony is abusing God's gift of food; greed is bending God's gift of abundance out of shape by hoarding and accumulating; and pleasure is overindulging God's gift of rest and all that is beautiful and pleasurable.

When the believer does not set limits, does not understand that all good things come from God and sin is simply the exploitation and overindulgent use of all that is good, then barrenness comes to the soul. Prayers that simply reinforce our passion for self-indulgence are prayers that will not be answered.

Friendship with the world. Jesus set the parameters for our involvement in the present world. He reminded us that we participate fully in the world, but in character we are not of the world (John 17:6ff). Friendship with the world is not a prohibition against being friendly with those we work or share a neighborhood with. To be a "friend of the world" means we adopt and accept the norms and values of the surrounding culture as our own. It means we dance to a drumbeat other than the Kingdom of God.

The church has made repeated attempts to ascertain worldliness through the making of rules — rules to control and govern what it means to be a friend of the world. Although it may be appropriate to give guidelines, the making of rules has not been a very satisfactory way to deal with worldliness.

Worldliness certainly means different things in different cultures, and to a lesser degree, it can also be different to each believer within the same culture and community of faith. It is very difficult to categorize all of life's experiences and initiatives as either godly or worldly. Teachers in the church must use great wisdom in helping believers sort out what belongs to God and what belongs to this age.

The pursuit of holiness. Personal holiness has two faces, each finding its source in different places. At the heart of holiness is the renewing and cleansing grace of God. In Jesus Christ, God declares the believer to be righteous and complete in him. This is the first and primary face of holiness.

The second face of holiness is the personal pursuit of Christlikeness to which every believer aspires. This is the process of becoming mature in the faith which God enables the believer to accomplish by diligent attention to life and sensitivity to the renewing, guiding presence of the Holy Spirit. And this is what James addresses in this text. The ten imperatives which he issues echo the Ten Commandments of the Old Testament (Ex. 20:1ff), except James' commands are a much more vigorous call to a devout and holy life.

Personal, practical holiness in the life of the Christian does not come without discipline and effort. It is a constant fight to submit to God, to resist the devil, to draw near to God and to humble oneself before God.

When truth becomes gossip, and gossip becomes slander. "The great sin of humanity is too much careless talking and not enough careful living!" writes James W. Kritchell. "The key to being tiresome is to tell all," intones Voltaire. James has not been afraid to tell it like it is. The truth concerning many matters has been spoken firmly and is frequently set into a hypothetical framework to protect specific persons from personal attack.

It is useful to make a distinction between truth being spoken in love and gossip. To speak the truth in love is always necessary and appropriate. But it must be done for the benefit and growth of the church. Gossip is talking too much; telling all when limits should be observed. Gossip is telling something about someone simply for the sake of telling it. It is the telling of a secret or a widely-known incident, not for the purpose of bringing healing and well-being to the person or event, but because curiosity and a meddlesome attitude drives it forward.

Slander is putting an uncharitable twist to a story so a person is wounded by the telling of it. Gossip is highly susceptible to becoming slander. The antithesis to gossip and slander is to control the tongue (3:1-12) and in Paul's words to have our speech be "full of grace, seasoned with salt" (Col. 4:6).

Personal Response

* Disagreements, quarrels and sniping are very much part of life. This happens in families, marriages, places of work and the church. There are quarrels and then there are quarrels. DISCUSS: Are all arguments equally wrong? Must all disagreements be destructive? Why does selfishness always change the tone of an argument to a more intense negative side?

* "Our 'needs' are always drawn from our list of 'wants'," declares Noel Barber. DISCUSS: Is this true? Is it good or bad, or does it simply reflect the trends of society?

* Worldliness is allowing the values and norms of the dominant culture to influence our way of thinking. DISCUSS: Is worldliness more attitude than action? Is it possible for two persons to do exactly the same thing and for one it is worldliness and for the other it is not?

* The key to spiritual well-being is submit to God, resist the devil and humble yourself before the Lord. DISCUSS: How does this work practically?

* James follows Jesus' teaching in issuing a prohibition against judging a brother/sister. DISCUSS: Why is this prohibition necessary?

CHAPTER TEN

The Fragility Of Life:
Caution! Proceed With Care!

Now listen, you who say, "Today or tomorrow we will go to this or that city, spend a year there, carry on business and make money." Why, you do not even know what will happen tomorrow. What is your life? You are a mist that appears for a little while and then vanishes. Instead, you ought to say, "If it is the Lord's will, we will live and do this or that." As it is, you boast and brag. All such boasting is evil. Anyone, then, who knows the good he ought to do and doesn't do it, sins.

Now listen, you rich people, weep and wail because of the misery that is coming upon you. Your wealth has rotted, and moths have eaten your clothes. Your gold and silver are corroded. Their corrosion will testify against you and eat your flesh like fire. You have hoarded wealth in the last days. Look! The wages you failed to pay the workmen who mowed your fields are crying out against you. The cries of the harvesters have reached the ears of the Lord Almighty. You have lived on earth in luxury and self-indulgence. You have fattened yourselves in the day of slaughter. You have condemned and murdered innocent men, who were not opposing you (James 4:13-5:6).

The Flow and Form of the Text

This is the fourth and final tirade against ungodly living which James hurls at his readers. The first three outbursts of strong, combative language were directed against the nasty, untamable speech of the tongue (3:1-12) against earthly, devilish wisdom which stands in opposition to heavenly wisdom (3:13-16) and against quarreling, conformity to the world, and slanderous, judgmental practice (4:1-12). The fourth tirade continues in the same tone and challenges the ethics of the business person.

James directs his words toward two issues, each introduced with "Now listen" (4:13; 5:1). In the first section, his comments are directed toward the itinerant entrepreneur who moves through the Roman world in search of trading business and profit. In the second section, James condemns the rich business entrepreneurial class who use their power to accumulate wealth by shortchanging those who work for them.

In typical fashion these texts are not only one-issue tirades. This is particularly true in 4:13-17. James' fertile mind moves rapidly from defining the issue, which is the entrepreneurial spirit of the rapid deployment of a business strategy to take advantage of a unique business opportunity (4:13) to making the case, because of the fragileness of life (4:14) that God ought to have a more central part in a person's daily plans (4:15) to a commentary on the nature of sin (4:17).

In 5:1-6 this tendency is not so evident but a more consistent and disciplined treatment of the subject material. Wealth and the entrepreneurial spirit are not condemned. What is condemned is the accumulation of wealth through dishonest means. This language is reminiscent of Old Testament prophetic speech where the judgment of God is pronounced with uncompromising power.

The Text Explained

Verses 13-17 address the routineness of life; that is, how the believer makes plans for living. In much of the planning for the routines of the day God is left on the sidelines. Since life is very fragile, each Christian ought to give more concentrated attention to this matter.

The business of living (vv. 13-14a) The business of living must be more than merely plotting the next strategy which will increase wealth. The issue is not whether business persons ought to plan for trading or plot the locality in which it will happen; rather it is whether Christians can do whatever they want without regard to God.

The background to James' thinking harks back to 1:2-8 where wise living is the central theme. To live wisely means to keep God centered into all of life, which is done by routine, everyday events. It encompasses speech, faith, good deeds, relationships in the church, as well as the business plans of entrepreneurs. To plan for business without realizing that all the days of our lives are in God's hands is to plunge ahead without being mindful of the Creator and Sustainer of all things. Paul the Apostle uses the phrase "if God wills" repeatedly to express his dependence on God (I Cor. 4:19; 16:7). He understood that life is fragile and all his plans remained subject to the will of God.

The fragility of life (v. 14b) The opening query, "What is your life?" is a universal question which calls each person to examine the nature and quality of life. James is not asking a philosophical question and expecting a complex answer. The answer he gives informs the reader what the intent of the question truly is. "You are a mist that appears for a little while and then vanishes" reminds every human being that nothing, particularly life, is forever.

This is a very familiar Old Testament theme. Isaiah likens life to the flowers and grasses of the field which wither in the hot wind and die (Is. 40:6-8). "Do not boast about tomorrow, for you do not know what a day may bring forth" (Prov. 27:1) is another way of saying the same thing. Jesus told the story of a man who made a fortune and decided to add to his barns and wealth so he could take up a life of ease and luxury, but unfortunately he forgot his soul would be required of him at some time (Luke 12:16-21).

Arrogance and cockiness are dreadful sins. In this text, the sin of planning life without God is exacerbated by the intent to brag and boast about one's accomplishments (4:16). In other words, the planning and scheming for profit in business ventures is fueled by the desire to boast about the success which is sure to come. Boasting and bragging are rooted in arrogance and a sense of invincibility. Conversely, living life under God's direction and understanding the role God plays in our lives makes us humble. Boasting about one's accomplishments suggests that God has had no part in the success. "All such boasting," James concludes, "is evil."

William Barclay wisely reminds us that while this text does warn against planning life without taking God into account, Christians ought not to be terrorized into fear and become paralyzed by inaction.   This text calls on us to commit all our plans into the hands of God and to live modestly with our successes and blamelessly with our failures.   This warning, communicated so powerfully by James, ought to flash its message clearly in every Christian's conscience: Caution! Life is fragile! Live it with care!

Redefining sin (v. 17) As with many parts of this epistle, James surprises the reader with an admonition which seems to come out of the dark.   "Anyone, then, who knows the good he ought to do and doesn't do it, sins" redefines sin from "action" to "intent". It is not only the things we do which defile us, it is also the things we should have done and did not do which contaminate us. The sin lies in the manner in which life is lived - that is, without regard to God in the planning and scheming of life - as well as in the intentional ignoring of what should have been done.

This redefinition of sin closely follows the teaching of Jesus who repeatedly argued that sin has an action-face and an attitude-face (Matt. 5:21-22; 27-28). James earlier wrote about the insidious, contaminating nature of sin. Sin is born when temptation gives entry to the sin which has lain in latent, dormant form and is turned into action. If temptation is not controlled, James argues, then sin invariably follows the pattern of childbirth: conception, incubation, giving birth and growing into full-grown actions (1:13-15).

Accumulating and scheming for wealth (vv. 1-6) The first paragraph which we have just examined has a whimsical tone to it. James the pastor seems to understand exactly how insidious sin truly can be. Sin intrudes into the very routines of life itself, contaminating the most common of all pursuits, even in the making of business plans so life can be sustained.

In 5:1-6 the tone changes dramatically. This is attributed to the nature of the subject material. There is something very intentional about the sins committed by the entrepreneurs who are described in this text. While the earlier paragraph warns against the danger of pushing God out of the center of life, here God is not only absent but is described as "the Lord Almighty" who hears the prayers and cries of the poor.

The ten sentences of this paragraph are ten exclamatory statements. They build a ten-step pyramid beginning with a command to "weep and wail" which literally means "to burst into uncontrolled weeping and howling with grief" (A.T. Robertson). The reason for the howling and weeping is because of the impending judgment of God.

Adding to the grief is the realization that the wealth, which has been pursued so relentlessly, is slowly disintegrating before their very eyes. It is becoming moth-eaten, rotten and corroded. Not only is it disintegrating into a worthless mass of junk but the growing junk pile itself stands as mute witness to the folly of having accumulated it. James once again stands squarely in the tradition of Jesus who assailed the same things (Matt. 6:19,24).

There are two levels of sinful behavior lodged in this paragraph. The first highlights the stupidity of spending all of life accumulating that which has no permanent value. Wealth is temporary, passing and has a very deceptive face.

The second level of sinful behavior is the abominable manner in which the wealth has been accumulated. It has been garnered on the backs of the poor from whom wages have been withheld. The phrase, "mowed your fields," indicates that the work for which they were hired was completed.

The parallels between this text and Old Testament prophetic judgment speeches are more than coincidence. James, who is steeped in Old Testament literature, was familiar with the laws which governed the relationship between worker and master. Wages were to be paid promptly (Lev. 19:13; Deut. 24:15); cheating, dishonest scales and false measures were forbidden (Lev. 19:35); and even the rights of the alien, the stranger in their midst, were protected by God from entrepreneurial injustice (Lev. 19:33-34).

The cries which "have reached the ears of the Lord Almighty" are consistent with the commands of the Lord Almighty to treat the poor, the disadvantaged, and the dislocated with respect and care (Micah 6:8). Earlier James has argued that religion which allows the widow and orphan to be ignored while in need is worthless religion (1:26-27). The accumulation of property and the centralization of wealth into the hands of a few rich landowners and the corrupting of the legal system to cover up these crimes is roundly condemned by God (Amos 5:11ff). Living in the lap of luxury while the poor, who have helped to produce the wealth, continue to live at a subsistent level of poverty recalls God's condemnation of Israel and provokes a just God to threaten the rich with impending judgment (Amos 6:1-7).

In a wonderfully ironic twist of Old Testament images, James uses "slaughter language" to reinforce the horrific sins of the rich. He accuses the rich of a self-indulgence which leads to fatness. Indeed, the problem with luxurious self-indulgent living is that it destroys fitness which decreases the potential for a good long life. Luxurious undisciplined living creates obese, lazy persons who are being "fattened ... for the day of slaughter."

To make an already severe indictment still more damning, James notes that these actions are tantamount to murder — not murder in an act of self-defence, but the murder of innocent men and women "who were not opposing you".

Application, Teaching/Preaching Points

The practical nature of the first paragraph and the powerful indictment of the rich in the second paragraph leads to many helpful application, teaching/preaching points. Five points stare at us from the text.

Be careful about planning life without God. God is very interested in every facet of our lives and wants to be part of everything in it. Through Jesus Christ, God is building a people of God who are to bear witness to their salvation by the life they live. To be a Christian means we live each day of our lives under the guidance, protection and sustaining hand of God.

The phrase "if God wills" should never be reduced to a trite religious slogan; rather, it ought to represent accurately the believer's intention for life. To use this phrase as a religious slogan without putting it into practice is to allow a split to develop between our words and our true intentions.

Caution! Proceed with care! Life is fragile! The span of life, the Psalmist opines, is seventy or, perhaps with good health, eighty years in duration (Ps. 90). In comparison with eternity, this is such a brief snitch of life that it can be described as a wisp of fog which the morning sun dissipates. If life is precious because it is short, if life is a gift and we do not know the span of our years, it ought to be lived richly and fully.

Furthermore, boasting about achievements vulgarizes life. Bragging is taking credit for those things which might not be exclusively of our own making. Many people contribute to our successes. God also has a part in these successes. Modesty is a wonderful gift. It allows credit for success to be shared. There can be nothing more boring and insufferable than having to listen to someone speak only of themselves and their accomplishments. Jesus himself noted that to speak of one's deeds with the intent to take credit for them ruins the possibility of receiving a reward from God (Matt. 6:5,16).

On doing and not doing good. This is a fertile application point for personal growth and teaching in the church. Sin is more than doing evil; sin is not doing the good we know we ought to do.

This pungent, clear statement on the nature of sin can be applied in either a negative or positive manner. Negatively, it can become a harangue against all of that which should have been done, but has not; positively, it can become a very powerful motivating influence for good. Usually it is more productive to use it as a motivational statement. If a deed is done out of fear, the person doing the good deed will find little joy in it; if the deed is done with happiness and joy, it usually is much more effective.

In the church community, great care must be taken not to create only a sense of failure and sinfulness. Such feelings of inadequacy don't need much encouragement. However, it also is wise to let the text (4:17) say exactly what it wants to say.

The accumulation of wealth at the expense of the poor is dirty wealth. The Scriptures teach that the poor, the powerless and the vulnerable ought not to be taken advantage of for economic gain. To exploit the weakness of the disadvantaged is to invoke the wrath of God. This is an inviolate principle of God and we dare not make it mean less than was intended. This is one side of the equation as we consider the application of this principle.

The other side of the argument is that we live in an increasingly global and complex world of commerce where the competitive edge of a business enterprise determines its success. Our society is structured in such a way that inefficient corporations and businesses go bankrupt and the efficient businesses continue to grow. Many of the jobs in this global economy require skilled labor. Increasingly, women and men are encouraged to upgrade skills in order to keep up with the rapid rate of change in the workforce. Those who can not compete or have few skills, or are older and not able to compete anymore are forced into the lower paying service industry jobs.

This economic reality requires considerable tact when applying this 2000-year-old word to our situation. The agrarian economy of the ancient Near East where dayworkers were hired to help plant the crop and gather the ripened harvest, is not the world most of us live in. Social justice issues in a day when cutbacks are common create much dislocation in the church community.

The principle must hold; that is, no disadvantaged person must be exploited for someone else's gain. Wages must be paid in full and on time. The accumulation of wealth for the sake of living a luxurious, self-indulgent life is not an acceptable practice.

The temporary nature of wealth. In James' day, wealth was symbolized by three commodities: metals like gold and silver, grains which fed the peoples of the known world, and fine apparel, silk and cloth traded throughout the Roman Empire. Indeed, a wealthy person was identified by two of these three commodities; the rings on his fingers and the fine clothes he wore (2:1-13). All three commodities are subject to decay and loss and their values are determined and enhanced only by the entrepreneurial acumen to keep them circulating. When James and Jesus note the temporary nature of wealth they were speaking at two levels: the first is the immediate time frame, and the second is when wealth is compared to a person's lifespan. Hoarding wealth is folly. It is to place too much confidence in that which has no lasting value.

Personal Response

* Planning is a central part of our lives. Schools, colleges, mission societies, businesses and individuals make strategic plans. Well-developed plans can be helpful to direct the energies of an institution, business or individual. DISCUSS: How important is it that every plan created be developed under the banner, "If the Lord wills and we live?" Is this a realistic way of doing strategic planning?

* While it is readily acknowledged that boasting and bragging is wrong, most human beings have a need to speak about their failures and successes. DISCUSS: Is it possible to speak about successes so it does not turn into self-serving boasting? Is it easier to speak about failures or success?

* The global economy means that most companies and businesses must compete in a larger marketplace than ever before. Jobs which once appeared to be secure have vanished. Large corporations determine so many of the working conditions and benefits which come to ordinary persons. DISCUSS: Are our entrepreneurs Christian business persons or are they business persons who happen to be Christian? Is there a distinction between these two options? What difference does it make if there is a distinction, or what is lost to the community of faith if there is no distinction?

* James is very bombastic and noisy with words when dealing with this subject. Sometimes he almost seems to be shouting. He paints a portrait of God as an angry taskmaster who will call for accountability from all business persons. DISCUSS: What do you think of this portrait of God? How do you see God?

CHAPTER ELEVEN

Bringing Belief And Lifestyle Together:
On Patience And Truthfulness

Be patient, then, brothers, until the Lord's coming. See how the farmer waits for the land to yield its valuable crop and how patient he is for the fall and spring rains. You too, be patient and stand firm, because the Lord's coming is near. Don't grumble against each other, brothers, or you will be judged. The Judge is standing at the door!

Brothers, as an example of patience in the face of suffering, take the prophets who spoke in the name of the Lord. As you know, we consider blessed those who have persevered. You have heard of Job's perseverance and have seen what the Lord finally brought about. The Lord is full of compassion and mercy.

Above all, my brothers, do not swear — not by heaven or by earth or by anything else. Let your "Yes" be yes, and your "No," no, or you will be condemned (James 5:7-12).

The Flow and Form of the Text

The form and tone of this epistle ebbs and flows in a series of waves. The first rush, focusing on wise living, begins with the abrupt opening of the epistle and sustains strong momentum throughout the first chapter. The material is diverse and topic after topic is explored with great passion and a minimum of words. This wave is characterized by a torrent of ideas, each idea just briefly brushed with words. Words which might describe this section are creative, imaginative, quick moving, interesting and free-association.

A second wave follows (2:1-26), although not quite as varied as the first. This consists of two in-depth homilies: a warning against prejudice in the church and the importance of works as a way of defining faith. Words describing this section are thoughtful, careful and penetrating.

The third wave (3:1-5:6) contains four intense, boisterous, noisy polemics. With loud and strident words, James rails against the tongue and careless speech, highlights two kinds of wisdom, discusses the nature of conflict in society and church, and presents a homily concerning the fragility of life and how it ought to be lived. The tone of this third wave is loud, noisy preaching at its most zealous level. Words to describe this wave are intense, strident, commanding and prophetic.

The fourth wave, which we will examine, changes the tone of the writing completely. It contains two major parts. It is quiet in tone, the pastoral word of the writer calling the community of believers to patience and prayer. In the earlier waves, the critical issue concerns how a believer is to choose between good and evil. Now James addresses those circumstances and issues which stand outside of the reach and choice of the scattered flock, circumstances of life that will not go away through any action of the individual.

Earlier a call is issued with clarion singleness to wise living, intentional living, and swimming against the tide of societal norms and values. Now the call is to a quietness before God, a waiting on the Eternal One to do that which only God can do. Hence the call is to patience and prayer.

The Text Explained

The passage before us consists of three paragraphs. The opening paragraph is a call to patience. All three paragraphs are addressed to "brothers" which, of course, means brothers and sisters. In these three paragraphs we are faced with the most pastoral, tender writing of the whole epistle. The subject of patience in the face of suffering is not something to be taken lightly. Pastoral counsel is always best received when there is a walking alongside those who need wisdom and patience, and wisdom never needs to shout.

Patience is a virtue (vv. 7-10) The first sentence begins with a command, "Be patient." The Greek word for patience *makrothumia* is a compound word; that is, it is two words pulled together to make one word. *Makro* means long, distant, far; *thumia* means anger. Therefore *makrothumia* (patience) literally means to live life with anger kept at a distance. The old, archaic English word "long-suffering" gets at this meaning a little better.

This waiting with anger under control is to last "until the Lord's coming." The quality of this patience is illustrated by the farmer who can do nothing but wait for the autumn and spring rains. Fretting does not help; being anxious does not produce rain. There is nothing to do but wait without anger welling up in the soul, to wait with anger kept at a distance, far away.

The command not to grumble and complain against each other flows from the call to be patient. The earlier text, where the cries and complaints of the poor reach up to the heavens where God lives, is a different kind of complaint (5:4). It is not wrong to complain about the unfairness of life which the injustices of society spawn. It is not wrong to pray to God about the trials and troubles which are part of life. Such complaints directed to God are in fact the prayers which God hears and answers. But it is wrong to complain and grumble against each other; that is, to grind at those who also share the present misery. God is the judge, James declares, and he is inclined to pass judgment on such irritating, untrusting behavior.

Suffering, though inevitable, is not a terminal condition (vv. 10-11) The second paragraph brings back an issue we have been introduced to before. In 1:2 the vexing trials created suffering. Now we have "suffering" named explicitly for the first time. It has been alluded to in many texts: it is assumed in the call to attend to the widows and orphans (1:26-27); although unspoken, it lies behind James' treatment of prejudice in the church (2:1-13); and it certainly intensifies the heavenward cries of the poor whose wages have been frozen by the rich landowners (5:4). To be sure, all of these people suffer, but now "suffering" is openly cited as the lot of the people of God who are scattered throughout the Roman Empire (1:1).

The Greek word *kakopathes* is a colorful word. It literally means bad (*kako*) pathos (*pathes*). Suffering has no value in itself. Suffering is a monstrous evil and stands in opposition to a rich, blessed life. Value does not lie in the act of suffering; rather, value lies in what suffering produces and accomplishes within the believer (5:11). Earlier (1:3-6) James argued that suffering, trials and hardships produce in us the ability to endure, which produces perfection so the believing person will lack nothing.

The examples for patient suffering are the prophets and saints of the Old Testament who endured amazing circumstances in the name of the Lord. James, who is conversant with the Old Testament, probably has those people in mind whom the writer of Hebrews lists (Heb. 11:1-40). The incredible legacy of these saints, together with prophets of the Old Testament, stands witness to the power of God to transcend the suffering of humanity.

The beatitude, which is introduced with "As you know, we consider ..." (and which incidentally ruins the classic form of the beatitude), is almost a repetition of the beatitude in 1:12. The context of the earlier, fuller beatitude is the fragility of life. Enduring ensures a "crown of life" from God. In the more abbreviated version of 5:11, blessedness is again attributed to those "who have endured". By repeating and reading the earlier beatitude into this text, James is reminding his hearers that God will reward those who suffer patiently in this life.

The introduction of the patriarch Job in this text reinforces the idea that most suffering is not of one's own making. Concerning the suffering which often arrives in life unannounced, one can do little; however, the manner in which a person responds to such events is very much in our hands.

"You have heard of Job's perseverance and have seen what the Lord finally brought about" has often been interpreted to mean Job was a patient man. Job in our text is not commended for his patience; he is commended for his perseverance, or endurance. The word endurance *hypomone* literally means "patient endurance" in whatever it is that is afflicting the believer.

The promise James holds out to those who suffer is that God can turn suffering into bliss. After all, God did it for Job. Although this sentence ought not to be interpreted as a sure guarantee that God will turn things around for all suffering persons like he did for Job, it nonetheless leans in that direction. The readers of this missive are to take courage and strength from God's interaction with the patriarch Job.

The concluding sentence, "The Lord is full of compassion and mercy," echoes Old Testament sentiments (Ps. 103, Jonah 4:1-3) and encourages the believer who is under the stress and duress of suffering to keep hope alive.

Truthfulness and integrity (v. 12) In the middle of a pastoral treatise on patience, suffering and perseverance James inserts a comment on truthfulness and personal integrity. This short two-sentence paragraph is the sixth and final comment on the problem of speech.

Connecting these comments requires a considerable leap; however, it seems what James has in mind is that suffering can place so much stress on believers they might be tempted to use double talk or even lies to avoid some suffering.

In this paragraph the pastoral tone once more gives way to the prophet. "My brothers" softens the commands somewhat. The content of the commands to let "yes" be yes and "no" be no closely follows on the words of Jesus who said exactly the same thing. Furthermore, the prohibition not to swear "by heaven or by earth or by anything else" is almost a direct quotation of Jesus (Matt. 5:33-37). While Jesus attributes the temptation to swear on objects to the Evil One (Matt. 5:37), James concludes his treatise on the swearing of oaths by announcing judgment, "you will be condemned" (5:12).

This strong prohibition and the announced judgment flows out of the Old Testament idea that truthfulness is the mark of being part of the people of God (Ex. 20:16).

Application, Teaching/Preaching Points

Strange as it might seem after having come through a bombastic, strident teaching section, there is finally a pastoral side to this epistle. Five pastoral bits of advice flow from this text, all of them necessary for a healthy, growing individual and church community.

Patience is a lifelong process and project. The command to be patient is to be expected. However, the duration of this patience is surprising; that is, "until the Lord returns." Eugene Peterson, in a helpful analysis of the Songs of Ascent in the Psalter, entitles his book, *A Long Obedience in the Same Direction* (Intervarsity Press, 1980). Probably one of the most significant and needful pastoral tasks in the church is to help believers develop the understanding that very few things are accomplished overnight, and building a Christian life is a lifelong process. Maturity comes slowly, sometimes even imperceptibly, but it does come. Suffering is rarely a short-term event, as it is part of life. Patience, keeping anger far away, is the first step in dissolving the disappointment and anger over those things which come to the Christian without cause.

Patience is helped by the promise of the Lord's return. In a recent visit to the Zairian church in Africa, some missions personnel were overwhelmed by the joyful expectation of the Lord's return in this suffering church. Heaven is very much on their mind. Suffering is made tolerable by the promise of eternal bliss. "The Lord is coming" is the rallying cry of the suffering church.

Patient waiting for the Lord's return and grumbling do not fit together. Since all believers await the return of the same Lord we should not be at each other's throats. Dissension, angry attitudes and words make waiting patiently much more difficult for everyone.

Be encouraged by the long list of role models available to the people of God. The Scriptures and post-biblical history are full of examples of women and men who endured shame and pain in the name of God. Sometimes when things are going poorly for individuals or for a whole church community, it seems as if the problems have never happened to anyone before. It is good to know that Christians walk in the tradition of many great women and men who have suffered greatly but endured to the end.

Many fine support ministries have developed as people who have experienced great loss and have come through the experience began to share with those in similar experiences. In the lonely hours of suffering even the stories of the biblical characters are of comfort to Christians.

Remember the Lord, the One who is compassionate and full of mercy. The Scriptures teach that Jesus Christ has suffered every temptation which we suffer, and there is no human experience which God has not seen or experienced. Compassion is a wonderful trait; it makes God accessible and mercy always draws us to God. Compassion is God's caring heart peering deeply and fully into the life of every believer, and mercy is God extending his care to the child of God. There are many role models for the church to follow, but care must be taken so that of all the role models available to the church for encouragement, Jesus Christ himself is not forgotten.

Personal integrity and truthfulness enhance the witness of suffering. To suffer for our own stupidity is an awful thing, but at least we know it is our own doing; to suffer for another's sake makes our suffering more complicated. The temptation to avoid suffering that is not of our own making might lead to a denial of the truth. If our "yes" is always yes and our "no" is always no, we will be known for our truthfulness and the witness of our faith will be enhanced. We ought never to use lies as a means to an end because the means is the end.

Truthfulness is the mark of being part of the people of God. Lying is attempting to adjust reality so something will be perceived differently than what it truly is. In the world outside of the community of faith, everything is not as it appears. Within the community of faith, however, the truth should be spoken in love and with openness.

Personal Response

* An old proverb says patience is a virtue. Patience can also be a curse. It is a virtue when everyone is rushing around frantically and no one wants to stop and reflect on the meaning of life. It is a curse when it allows things to be left undone which should be done. DISCUSS: When is patience a virtue and when is patience a curse? How does a Christian sort out when to be patient and when to be active?

* Grumbling and complaining is almost a national pastime. A national newsmagazine called North Americans "the most com-

plaint-happy" society in the world. It is not that we are such an unhappy lot, we just complain a lot. Grumbling also has a corrosive effect on the church. DISCUSS: Why do you think grumbling comes so easily to us? Is grumbling a sign of discontentment or is it just a bad habit?

* The patriarch Job is a most interesting character. He survived his trauma, so he certainly is a minority. DISCUSS: Do you think Job is a good role model for endurance? What can we learn from Job other than simply enduring?

* Truth-telling is the mark of being a Christian. DISCUSS: Can you think of some incidents or times when, in order to protect someone, the truth ought not to be spoken? Is truthfulness only not telling lies, or is it also withholding a part of the truth?

CHAPTER TWELVE

The Key To Wellness:
Persistence In Prayer

Is any one of you in trouble? He should pray. Is anyone happy? Let him sing songs of praise. Is any one of you sick? He should call the elders of the church to pray over him and anoint him with oil in the name of the Lord. And the prayer offered in faith will make the sick person well; the Lord will raise him up. If he has sinned, he will be forgiven. Therefore confess your sins to each other and pray for each other so that you may be healed. The prayer of a righteous man is powerful and effective.

Elijah was a man just like us. He prayed earnestly that it would not rain, and it did not rain on the land for three and a half years. Again he prayed, and the heavens gave rain, and the earth produced its crops.

My brothers, if one of you should wander from the truth and someone should bring him back, remember this: Whoever turns a sinner away from his error will save him from death and cover over a multitude of sins (James 5:13-20).

The Flow and Form of the Text

The final pericope of this epistle ends as abruptly as it opened. It began with a torrent of words giving counsel in wise living, and it ends with a torrent of words concerning the problems which beset individual persons — the problems common to humanity which tend to not go away without divine help.

This text consists of three paragraphs and in typical fashion is written in a terse manner. The first paragraph is characterized by three simple questions, each highlighting a personal problem or circumstance in life. The first two questions are answered in very concise, straightforward language. The third question is given a much more detailed, ordered and programmed answer. This is the only New Testament text which gives a step-by-step solution to the problem of pain and the healing power of God.

In other New Testament texts, the promises of answered prayer are much more general and are not directed specifically toward the healing of the body. For example, Jesus told his disciples that "the Father will give you whatever you ask in my name" (John 15:16), and "if you have faith as small as a mustard seed, you can say to this mountain, 'Move from here to there' and it will move. Nothing will be impossible for you!" (Matt. 17:20).

The second paragraph is an illustration to reinforce the need for earnest, believing prayer. Again, as with all other illustrations in this epistle, the story is from a well-known Old Testament personality.

The third paragraph is the concluding statement of the epistle. It introduces a topic which has not been raised before. And as quickly as it is raised, it is dropped. And with the dropping of this remarkable new theme, the epistle ends. It ends abruptly and without any greetings or farewells.

The Text Explained

This final section draws on the background of the wisdom literature of the Old Testament where a balanced view of life is presented. The Book of Proverbs presents life in terms of actions and consequences; that is, every action in life has a corresponding consequence. Therefore, whatever is present in our lives is there because it is the natural consequence of how we have lived our lives. If we live well and do good, good will come to us; conversely, if we live poorly, terrible things will befall us. Proverbs is a supreme book of common sense sayings, and most of the times it works quite well. The patterns usually hold quite firmly.

The Book of Job tells another story. Job lives well. He regularly brings an offering to God on behalf of himself and his children. He is blameless and serves God faithfully. Terrible trouble comes into his life and it is not of his making. Job's friends are sure there must be a connection between his suffering and the way he has lived in the past. Job, of course, protests his innocence and is not aware of the conversation between God and the Devil.

The problem which Job's life raises is that conventional wisdom, as postulated by Proverbs, does not always work. The question behind Job's story is this: how do we handle the terrible things that happen to us when they are not of our making?

The musings of the Book of Ecclesiastes go in exactly the opposite direction from the trials and life of Job. The preacher's problem is that everything works too well. The pattern never changes. Each human being is caught in an endless pattern of repeating events and life is boring and dull. How does a person sustain interest in life when everything is set into routines and patterns that are unchanging? So it does not surprise us that the preacher, the author of the book, thinks most of life is simply "a chasing after the wind" (Ecc. 1:14).

This passage, written with great pastoral compassion, is to the Epistle of James what Job is to Old Testament wisdom literature. James earlier assured the believer that God will hear and answer the prayer prayed in unwavering faith. Now James answers the query about what happens when sickness and pain come into the life of the believer.

Three questions; three answers. This first paragraph opens with three questions. It is amazing how simply James answers the first two questions. "Is any one of you in trouble?", James' simple answer is, "He should pray." We have met this word "trouble" *kakopathes* before (5:10) where it is translated as suffering. The word literally means "bad pathos". It describes the misfortune that comes into someone's life, often the routine misfortune which afflicts everyone.

James' surprising answer, "He should pray," indicates the believer is to expect these troubles. Many of them are there because that is how life happens. Prayer, speaking to God, is the perfect antidote to the troubles which are part of the routineness of life.

James has covered this material earlier (1:2-8). Does the believer need wisdom to keep God central in things when life is full of trials and trouble? Of course! And wisdom comes through asking God for it (1:5).

The second question, "Is anyone happy?" is also answered with a surprisingly simple answer, "Let him sing songs of praise." It was the custom of the first century congregations to sing praises to God in their corporate gatherings. Paul refers to such worship when he encourages the Ephesian congregation to "Speak to one another with psalms, hymns and spiritual songs. Sing and make music in your heart to the Lord, always giving thanks to God the Father for everything in the name of our Lord Jesus Christ" (Eph. 5:19-20). Jesus chastised the Pharisees, saying, "We played the flute for you and you did not dance; we sang a dirge and you did not mourn" (Matt. 11:17).

The third question, "Is any one of you sick?" requires a more disciplined answer. James gives a comprehensive step-by-step pattern for the practice of the prayer of healing.

Three specific comments mark this event. First, the process is to be centered in the congregational life of the afflicted person and flows to the sick person from the leadership of the local congregation. "Call the elders" has two nuances: it is the mature leadership of the local congregation who should be involved in this healing event; and for protection from abuse by the hucksters of religion who promise healing, it is to be the known and called-out elders of the community of faith who are to pray the prayer of faith. Hucksters who peddle religion and healings for a fee appear to have been part of the first century world. Peter confronts such a charlatan who wanted the gift of healing for economic gain (Acts 8:9-25).

The second comment, "to pray over him" means that individualized attention is centered on the afflicted person. The prayers are to be focused and are to center on the healing of the person.

Third, "anoint him with oil in the name of the Lord" is to protect a people from beginning to believe that the oil in itself might have some magical power. Oil in the Old Testament is a symbol of blessing or consecration (Ex. 40:13; I Sam. 10:1; 16:13); in the New Testament it is a metaphor to describe the readiness which prepares a person to enter eternal bliss (Matt. 25:1-13). It is not the oil which heals, although it is clear that oil in Jesus' day was thought to have medicinal value. Ultimately it is God who heals through the prayer of faith "in the name of the Lord".

The unilateral promise, "And the prayer offered in faith will make the sick person well; the Lord will raise him up," is a very strong statement of assurance and follows other New Testament promises of an unequivocal answer from God (John 15:16; Matt. 17:20). The word used to describe the healing, "will make well," literally means "to save, to deliver, to heal," and is the common New Testament word usually associated with salvation. However, salvation of the soul is not what is in focus here.

The problem with this unequivocal promise is that not all persons are healed physically when they are prayed over. While the verb, "will make well," which is a future tense, active voice verb, seems to cover more than only physical healing of the body, it must be granted that physical healing is the primary focus of this text. The context of the prayer of faith is the question, "Is any among you sick?"

"If he has sinned, he will be forgiven" ties together the healing of the body with the forgiveness of sins. The ancient world, much more than the present world, tied sins and illness together even though the experience of Job and Jesus himself (Mark 2:1-12) debunked the theory that illness is always the result of specific sin (see John 5:1-15; 9:1-41). Jesus, however, in the same narrative heals both the paralytic and forgives his sins.

That there is a connection between our sins and the healing of our bodies is established by the next sentence: "Therefore confess your sins to each other and pray for each other so that you may be healed." This should not surprise us at all. Throughout the Jewish community and the early Christian church, the idea that confession of sins ought to be made not only to God but also to our fellow human beings was a common idea. Jesus even went so far as to say, "whatever you shall bind on earth shall be bound in heaven, and whatever you shall loose on earth shall be loosed in heaven" (Matt. 16:19) pointing out that the leaders of the community of faith also have a role in declaring a person free from sin. Of course, it is God and not human beings who forgives sins.

It is always easier to confess our sins to God than it is to confess them to other people. Sin creates at least two barriers: a barrier between God and ourselves, and a barrier between us and our fellow human beings. Both barriers must be dismantled. Jesus illustrated the removal of these barriers when he told the story of a young lad who left home with anger in his heart and a good time on his mind (Luke 15:11-32). He squandered all his wealth, and upon returning home knew instinctively he had to confess his sins to both God and his father. His words, "I have sinned against heaven and against you" (Luke 15:21), opened the way for the healing of broken relationships.

Elijah, a man of like passion and prayer (vv. 17-18) The clinching sentence of the previous paragraph, while ending the discourse on how healing prayers are to be ordered, is also the opening sentence to introduce Elijah as a person effective in prayer. While it is understood that righteousness and effective praying go hand in hand, it is to be understood that not only great and famous people can be "powerful and effective" in prayer.

The paragraph opens with the comment that Elijah was a man "of like passion", a person "just like us" (NIV). However, as he is most well-known for the shutting up of the heavens so no rain might fall, the Mount Carmel confrontation with King Ahab and the priests of Baal, and the deluge of rain that followed (I Kings 17-18), Elijah seems to be set apart from ordinary people. But when the whole story of Elijah is known, including his stay with the widow of Zarephath and the dreadful loneliness and fatigue after his confrontation with King Ahab, he becomes a much more ordinary person.

In other words, it is a righteous person who has high points and low moments — a person who is kept alive either by ravens which are sent from God or in the home of a widow who shares her meager food stuffs, a person who stands, one day, triumphantly before God and a people and the next day sits under a tree awash in fatigue and self pity — it is such a person who is righteous, who prays and receives an answer from God.

Final things (vv. 19-20) James concludes this epistle with the same abruptness as he started. Here James introduces a theme which appears nowhere else in his writing. He opens the paragraph with a final "My brothers", the twelfth such address, and introduces the matter of "wandering from the truth". The wandering *planao* literally means to go astray. The sense of the word describes a wandering which is not so much a denial of the truth but a going astray by not giving attention to those things which keep one in the faith. To gently return such people to the faith, to make such people see the error of their wandering, will save them from death and will cover their sins.

What a wonderful way to end a book. To call the church to redemptive action, to have people of God looking for the erring ones and drawing them back into the Christian community is to be truly doing the work of God.

Application, Teaching/Preaching Points

This final group of paragraphs are a very practical call for the church to be active in all facets of the believer's life. It covers five major areas of ministry. A healthy Christian and a vibrant church community will give attention to these matters.

A praying community. Prayer is central to the life of the church. On one hand Jesus warned that the prayers spoken in public ought not to be done for public recognition (Matt. 6:5-8); rather God hears the prayers which are spoken in the stillness of the private place. On the other hand, Jesus also noted that "where two or three are gathered in my name" he is present with them (Matt. 18:20).

This passage teaches that we ought not to set any limits on the power of prayer. Through prayer our troubles, our *kakopathes* (bad pathos), are put into perspective, our bodies are healed and our sins are forgiven. We are to pray for each other, not neglecting to name the people and issues which need the guiding hand of God.

A singing, worshipping community. Happiness is best expressed through joyful singing. The people of God are a Good News people, living in the shadow of the cross and in the reality of the resurrection. Darkness and the power of darkness have been overwhelmed by Jesus, the Light of the world. The cultural barriers which have divided society have come down in the church. Rich and poor, educated and uneducated, widows, orphans, landowners, day laborers and business entrepreneurs all sit together, offering a cacophony of praise to God.

A story is told about an incident in Rwanda when refugees were streaming into Zaire. They were running in fear of their lives. Cholera was rampant, children and adults were dying, food was scarce, and sanitary conditions were abominable. In the midst of such horror a Christian family, barely clinging to life, began to sing. Others joined in. It never developed into a grand choir of praise to God but for a few hours these hungry, frightened souls were lifted from the bleakness of the terror which beset them and transformed it into something uplifting and beautiful.

A healing community. One of the outstanding characteristics about the early church was being a healing church. The early church fathers report that the gift of healing was a well-practiced gift in the church. Paul lists the gift of healing as one of the gifts bestowed on the church (I Cor. 12:9). The church has always attended to the sick and disadvantaged. James has argued repeatedly that the sign of authentic Christian faith is that it cares for the disadvantaged (1:27-28), refuses to discriminate against the poor (2:1-13) and pays attention to those who suffer (5:13-16).

Sadly, with the advent of the social welfare state and modern medicine, healing through the prayer of faith no longer holds a central place in the church. To a large degree, the church has relegated the healing process to the practice of medicine, and with considerable success. However, while every Christian applauds the advances of modern medicine, the church ought to be active in the laying on of hands, anointing with oil, and offering the prayer of faith for the healing and well-being of the total person.

A forgiving community. This passage ties together the healing of the body and the forgiveness of sins. Much care must be observed so the people of God do not think that all illness is tied to sinfulness. Some illnesses are simply part of our humanness. However, there is a connection between the sinful attitudes and behaviors which afflict humanity and the illnesses which consume our bodies. Some behaviors, such as excessive eating, drinking of alcohol, smoking tobacco products, and other such practices have consequences which result in illness. Attitudes such as bitterness, resentment, unresolved anger and worry also produce illness. The healing and cleansing of the body and soul of such destructive behaviors are part of the healing process.

This passage reminds us that the prayer of faith for the healing of a person must also be a time of confessing sins, both to God and to our fellow human beings. There are few moments in life when people are so open to God as when illness has come. It is important that church leadership recognizes the great opportunity for healing both the body and the spirit.

A seeking, forgiving community. The community of faith is a watchful community. Watchfulness has both an internal and external nature. James wrote this epistle to help foster a balanced, ordered Christian life. Its message is aimed at the believing person. In this passage attention is focused on those who wander from the faith. A healthy church will always be alert to those who are wandering or drifting away from the faith community. A church which pays little attention to the ones who are straying will also be a church which pays little heed to the ethical life of the congregants.

To seek and find those who are in the process of losing themselves in the world is to save a person from death. To "cover a multitude of sins" is another way of saying the church must be a forgiving community. To withhold forgiveness is to frustrate the grace of God.

Personal Response

* Prayer is the life line which connects a believer to the Lord. Prayer has to do with expectations: that is, if we have no expectations from God, then we will have little to pray about; conversely, if we have great expectations of God, we will be much more intense and disciplined in our prayers. DISCUSS: It has been argued that "scared people, people with few options, pray the best." Do you agree?

* Modern medicine and prayer belong together. The advances of modern science are part of God's common grace to us. DISCUSS: Is the prayer of faith for healing only a last resort or should it be practiced much more openly in the church?

* Elijah was a man "just like us." He prayed and God answered mightily. In other texts (Matt. 15:21-28) it is the little faith which is rewarded with an answer. DISCUSS: What does it take for God's healing power to come to us? Does it take much faith or little faith?

* Many of us have grown up in a tradition where sins are confessed to God, unless they have been specifically directed toward an individual. Public confession of sins is not readily practiced or easily understood in many of our congregations. DISCUSS: How broadly should sins be acknowledged and confessed?

* To bring drifting, wandering persons back to the faith is an ongoing need in the church. DISCUSS: What is the answer to help arrest the drifting process which seems to be part of each congregation's history?

CHAPTER THIRTEEN

Final Things:
A Theology Of The Epistle of James

Why do We Need Theology?

David Ewert, quoting a great British essayist, observes, "We are constantly being told that churches are empty because preachers insist too much on doctrine, dull dogma. The fact is the precise opposite. It is the neglect of dogma that makes for dullness. The Christian faith is the most exciting drama that ever staggered the imagination of humanity, and dogma is the drama" (from unpublished sermon).

The church lives by truth. Knowledge of God is central to understanding ourselves and the world in which we live. Misinformation always leads to disaster. The Scriptures warn believers to build carefully on the foundation that has been put in place — a foundation which is Jesus Christ (I Cor. 3:10-15). We study the Scriptures because Jesus said, "The words that I have spoken to you are spirit and life" (John 6:63).

Doctrine or dogma are the words we use to describe the teachings of the Scriptures on a certain subject. Doctrinal statements can also be called summary statements; that is, they summarize and bring together all the teaching of the Scriptures on a given subject. The usefulness of such summary statements is obvious even to the most casual reader of the Bible.

Of course too much theological musing in the past history of the church has led to an endless, sterile, philosophical debate about abstract issues that have little to do with how the Christian life is lived. But this is not the only kind of theology that exists. Properly understood theology is thinking the thoughts of God, understanding the wisdom and counsel of God, and learning to know the God who is the Lord of history. This kind of theology is anything but boring.

The goal of theology is to lead the believer to live a fuller, richer Christian life. Paul warned the early church about spinning endless words and becoming mesmerized by myths and controversies which abound in every culture but do not lead to maturity (I Tim. 1:3-7).

The Epistle of James is full of commands to live a rich, godly life and is easily summarized into a biblical theology. This particular chapter is not intended to compare the teachings of James to other biblical writers; rather it is intended to organize its material into subject groupings so the wide diversity of the epistle is more easily understood.

James presents the reader with a most stimulating and interesting theology. What makes it so appealing is the various levels of thinking which are presented. Some important subjects are simply brushed, lightly touched with words, while other subjects are plumbed to great depths. In some cases, a subject is unraveled like an onion, layer after layer, until the core of the subject matter is established.

A Theology of the Epistle of James

The inevitability of trials. Trials are simply part of life. They can not be avoided and they come in many different shapes and sizes (1:2). The inevitable trials which come to the believer must not be seen as temptations; that is, solicitations to participate in sinful behaviors. Although trials are part of life and come to the believer through ordinary events, they should not be interpreted as coming from God. They do not originate in God because God is good and all of his creative works are good (1:13).

This epistle gives many different illustrations of the kinds of trials that beset the Christian community. Some trials have to do with a believer's economic position in society. Some people are poor and are discriminated against within the church community

(2:1-4). Others are day laborers and are afflicted by the whims of the rich (5:4-6). Still others suffer because of their circumstances in life (5:10). And since all believers will eventually die, some trials are physical in nature (5:14-16).

The nature of sin. Although this epistle is very concerned with the ethical lifestyle of the Christian, and James is very noisy in his condemnation of loose living, he does not endlessly flog sinfulness in detail. James does, however, go to considerable lengths to outline the process through which each person moves from the first hint of sin, which is a thought, to the final end of sin which is death. In this it adds much important information on the nature of sin, because it is one of very few New Testament texts which addresses this subject.

Sin has both an intentional side and an inadvertent side. Sin is born deeply within the mind of each person. It begins with a thought. What makes the thought dangerous is it strikes a responsive chord within a person. Giving assent to this responsive note puts in place the intention to act on the idea. When the idea leads to an action, sin has been fully formed in our mind. Sin is putting into practice that which we have given assent in our minds. The final end of sin is death (1:14-15).

But sin is not only defined by the actions which are born in our thoughts. Sin is not only bringing into action those things which satisfy our evil desires, it is also <u>not bringing into action</u> those things we ought to be doing (4:17).

In this writing sin always involves the mind. At one time it is following our evil impulses; at other times it is ignoring our noble impulses. And since sin is always sin, it matters little to God whether sin is doing bad things or if it is only ignoring the good things that ought to be done. In God's sight all sin is equal because to break the law, the moral code of behavior, in just one point makes the person guilty of breaking it all (2:10).

Certain acts in the epistle, while not being labeled specifically as sin, are roundly condemned as being sinful. Worthless religion (1:26-27), favoritism (2:1-13), an out-of-control tongue (3:1-12), fighting and quarreling (4:1-3), cheating day laborers (5:1-6) and grumbling (5:9) are sinful behaviors and come under the judgment of God. Even James cautions, "This should not be" (3:10).

The character of God. James gives the reader a rather thorough exposition on the character of God. God is portrayed as the supreme giver of wisdom (1:5). The wisdom from God, or heaven, is the opposite of the wisdom of this world which is full of chaos and disorder (3:13-18). His giving is characterized by generosity and openness. Although God will use the trials of life as a forge to shape and perfect the life of the believer, God is not the author of sin nor tempts anyone with sin (1:13). God is good, therefore every gift which comes from him is good (1:17). Furthermore, in God there is such consistency of purpose and such quality of being that there is no variableness in his brightness and no shadows in his being (1:17).

God is a prime mover in our salvation giving us new birth (1:18) and his plan for us is we should live a righteous life (1:20). At the end of our life, God becomes a rewarder of those who have lived well (1:12).

God has created a new community of people who are to reflect his purposes. Therefore God cannot abide discrimination in the church (2:1-13) and will judge the willfully recalcitrant. On the other hand, God is merciful and forgiving (2:13) and full of compassion (5:11).

God is the healer (5:14) and the hearer of our most anguished cries and prayers. He hears the cries of the oppressed (5:1-6) and the prayers of those who, like Elijah, are righteous, intense and upright (5:16).

God is the Lord Almighty (5:4) the Lord who is coming from heaven (5:7-9) the One who comes near to us when we draw near to him (4:8) the One who is the Judge (4:12) and our Lord and Father (3:9).

Wisdom: keeping God centered in life. This epistle has a great deal to say about wise living. It acknowledges that each believer needs wisdom from God to live life decently (1:5). This wisdom is in competition with the wisdom which has its origins in the devil (3:15-16). Each person on earth is controlled either by the wisdom of this world or heavenly wisdom. The wisdom that comes from God issues in a life full of goodness, purity, peace, kindness and gentleness. This stands in opposition to worldly, earthly wisdom which is fraught with evil, selfish ambition and disorder.

The key to finding such wisdom is twofold: first, it is available from God and requires asking in faith (1:5-8); and second, it comes when the Christian, in a very intentional way, flees the advances of the devil and draws near to God (4:7-8).

Keeping God centered in life is recognizing God's pervading presence in all circumstances and plans of life, and acknowledging this presence by living life under the byline, "If God wills" (4:15).

A new people: finding a place to stand. The people called by God into the community of faith are to be different from the people who make up society. This new society is a people where the humble, common folk are exalted, and the rich and powerful "take pride in [their] low position" (1:9-11). In other words, the Christian community turns the values and norms of society on its head and inaugurates a new society where each person finds dignity and a place to stand.

This destroys all discrimination. The "poor man in shabby clothes" and the "man wearing fine clothes" are to be seated side-by-side without regard to outer appearance (2:1-13). At the heart of this new way of living is Jesus' word, quoted from the Old Testament, you shall "love your neighbor as yourself" (2:8).

Further, this new community is a worshipping, praying community. It is the place where joyful singing is practiced, where believing prayer is spoken, where sins are confessed and physical ailments are healed (5:13-18). It is a community of faith where the erring ones are encouraged to return to the faith (5:19-20).

Good works: the sign of a vibrant, confessing faith. Probably the most controversial teaching of this epistle has to do with the relationship between faith and works (2:14-26). Largely because of the contemporary preoccupation with the conflict between Paul and James, we have missed the heart of the teaching of James on this subject. This is too bad for the church.

James opens his treatment of the subject with the candid admission that religion which only talks a good talk and proclaims a great faith but is barren of good works is a bogus faith. James is concerned with the plight of the widow and orphan (1:26-27), the stranger who, in great need, arrives at our door (2:14-17), and the business entrepreneur who delays paying day laborers for their work (5:1-6).

Authentic faith must not only be proclaimed by words but must also deal with social justice matters with great fairness. Good deeds are the measuring stick of faith: that is, no good deeds, no faith; many good deeds, vibrant faith. Given this understanding between faith and good works, James can reinterpret the life and actions of Abraham the patriarch and Rahab the prostitute.

Endurance: the way to eternal bliss. The Epistle of James is quite heavenly minded. It calls attention again and again to the judgment of God at the end of the age. This present age is to be characterized by an endurance which knows no end. Endurance is the ability to take what life gives without shrinking into the background or giving up the belief in a good God. Endurance is rewarded with the crown of life (1:12). It produces perfection within us so the Christian will be complete, lacking nothing (1:4). Endurance is the key to patient living (5:11). Endurance is not a fatalistic resignation to the realities which are part of life; it is the triumphant bearing of the load so good qualities can be born in our lives (1:5-8).

Judgment: God is involved in life. This epistle is full of judgment language. Sometimes the references are to the end-time judgment of God; other times it is reminding believers of what is acceptable behavior and what is not acceptable.

Three specific texts describe circumstances and events which come under the judgment of God. In 1:9-11 judgment is described by using a metaphor common to the Scriptures. The grasses of the fields and the flowers of the meadows are burned to a crisp by the hot desert sun. The rich will fade as surely as the flowers will wilt and die. In 1:26-27 a twofold judgment is pronounced on religion which does not practice good deeds. First, such religion is particularly susceptible to self-deception and is dangerous because it thinks it is valid when it is a bogus faith; and second, such religion is pronounced to be worthless. In 4:4 the issue is being intimate with the world which sets the person against God; that is, to be an enemy of God which is "hatred of God".

In these three texts the believer is under judgment, but it is not only an end-time judgment; rather, James asserts that such behaviors also have implications for how life is presently being lived.

In five other texts, the judgment seems to be an end-time event. In 2:12 it appears that all persons will eventually be judged either by the law which gives freedom, or by the lack of mercy which has characterized a person's life on earth. In 3:1 James argues a more stringent end-time judgment will be exacted of teachers than of other church participants, although it has present implications as well. In 4:12 James names the One we will have to face, the One who is the judge; that is, there is one Lawgiver and one Judge. In 5:5 "You have fattened yourselves in the day of slaughter," appears to be very much an end-time judgment. And in 5:9 "The Judge is standing at the door!" is a reminder that all of our actions and attitudes are subject to the scrutiny of the Eternal One.

Words, words and still more words. The Epistle of James presents the church with a comprehensive New Testament treatment on the subject of words and the tongue. Words, their use and abuse, is not a dominating, major theme in the New Testament. In the Old Testament, however, a thorough development of the theme is found in the Book of Proverbs. Walter Dale, in an introductory sermon to James, called it "the wisdom literature of the New Testament". He is partially correct in this comment as Proverbs is concerned with right behavior so right living will be practiced. The Epistle of James is also concerned with right living, but that is where the similarities end. While Proverbs is a collection of pithy sayings on many different subjects, this epistle is much more ordered and disciplined, and is rooted in the sayings and life of Jesus Christ. While most of the Proverbs are good common sense sayings, James roots his writings in the theological life of the new community of faith which stands as a witness to the reign of God in the world.

The centerpiece of James' thinking is 3:1-12, where three distinct points are made. First, the tongue has incredible power for destruction; second, it is restless and virtually untamable; and third, in spite of all this, it is the instrument we use to bless God and curse humanity.

Anger and angry words do not promote "the righteous life that God desires" (1:20). Empty words that are not backed up with action are worthless and self-deceiving words (1:26-27); words that pronounce the blessing of God as an escape from social responsibility are dreadful words (2:16); quarreling words and fighting words are rooted in selfishness (4:1-3); words that exclude God from business plans or words that are boastful push God away from the center of life (4:13-16); words that are used to swear oaths rather than stating the truth destroy our credibility (5:12); and words that are vehicles of prayer, singing and confessing sins (5:13-18) are words that honor God and build the church.

Words, James argue, are so central to all of life that they mirror our innermost spirit and values. A Christian ought to reflect the new life of faith by the manner in which words are used.

James and Jesus: the epistle and Matthew's Gospel. Even to the most casual reader of the epistle, the strange absence of Jesus Christ from the narrative, except for the two occasions (1:1; 2:1), is easily observed. While this absence is noted in almost every writing on this letter, the close relationship between the Gospel of Matthew and the Epistle of James is also noted. Standing in the shadows of almost every section of the text are the words of Jesus. Ralph Martin suggests there are twenty-three such parallels. Listed below are some of the more obvious examples of these comparisons.

Rejoice in trials	James 1:2	Matthew 5:12
Ask God and he will give	James 1:5	Matthew 7:7
Blessed are those who endure	James 1:12	Matthew 24:13
Do not judge	James 2:13	Matthew 6:14-15
On oaths	James 5:12	Matthew 5:33-37
On hoarding	James 5:2-3	Matthew 6:19
On anger	James 1:20	Matthew 5:22
On slander	James 4:11	Matthew 5:22
On words without deeds	James 2:14-16	Matthew 7:21-23
Blessing the poor	James 2:5	Matthew 5:3
Warnings against the rich	James 2:6-7	Matthew 19:23-24
Helping the poor	James 2:16	Matthew 25:35
The prophets	James 5:10	Matthew 5:12

It is often argued that the Epistle of James is weakened in its impact because it is more God-centered than Christ-centered. It must be conceded that the overt Christological content is rather weak when compared, for example, to the letters Paul wrote. However, a closer reading of the text and the overwhelming reliance of James on the very words of Jesus makes this writing much more Christological than it first appears.

Final Things

This epistle, which had such a hard time finding its way into the biblical canon, is truly God's living word to the church. It is concerned about Christian living. Its burden is to bring belief and lifestyle together. It is concerned that the new community of faith will live the Christian life fully and richly and that each person, regardless of status in life, will find acceptance and the necessary strength to live in unity while "scattered among the nations" (1:1).

Motyer, Alec. *The Tests of Faith*. Downers Grove: IVP, 1970

Reicke Bo. *The Epistles of James, Peter and Jude*. The Anchor Bible. New York: Doubleday, 1964

Rienecker, Fritz. *A Linguistic Guide to the Greek New Testament*. Vol. II. Grand Rapids: Zondervan, 1980

Robertson, A.T. *Word Pictures in the New Testament*. Vol. IV. Nashville: Broadman, 1933

Sidebottom, E.M. *James, Jude and II Peter*. The New Century Bible Commentary. Grand Rapids: Eerdmans, 1967

Stulac, George M. *James*. IVP New Testament Commentary Series. Downsers Grove: IVP, 1993

Williams, R.R. *The Letters of John and James*. The Cambridge Bible Commentary. Cambridge: University Press, 1965

BIBLIOGRAPHY

Adamson, James B. *The Epistle of James.* New International Commentary on the New Testament. Grand Rapids: Eerdmans, 1976

Adamson, James B. *James, the Man and His Message.* Grand Rapids: Eerdmans, 1989

Barclay, William. *The Letters of James and I Peter.* Edinburgh: Saint Andrews Press, 1958

Brown, Colin, ed. *New Testament Theology.* Grand Rapids: Zondervan, 1967

Davids, Peter. *Commentary on James.* New International Greek Testament Commentary. Grand Rapids: Eerdmans, 1982

Davids, Peter. *James.* New International Biblical Commentary. Peabody, Mass: Henrickson, 1983

Dibelius, Martin. *James.* Hermeneia. Revised by Heinrich Greeven. Philadelphia: Fortress, 1976

Hiebert, D. Edmond. *The Epistle of James: Tests of a Living Faith.* Chicago: Moody, 1979

Kittel, Gerhard. *Theological Dictionary of the New Testament.* Translated by Geoffrey W. Bromiley. Grand Rapids: Eerdmans, 1964

Manton, Thomas. *James.* Crossway Classic Commentaries. Wheaton: Crossways, 1995

Martin, Ralph P. *James.* Word Biblical Commentary. Waco: Word, 1988

Mayor, Joseph B. *The Epistle of St. James.* Twin Books Series. ,Grand Rapids: Baker, 1978 reprint of 1897 edition

Moo, Douglas J. *James.* Tyndale New Testament Commentaries. Grand Rapids: Eerdmans, 1985

Motyer, Alec. *The Message of James.* The Bible Speaks Today. Downers Grove: IVP, 1985